Signwritten Art

SIGNWRITTEN ART

A·J·LEWERY

DAVID & CHARLES
Newton Abbot   London

Ellesmere Port, Cheshire, about 1910.
(Boat Museum Trust Reference Library, E.P.)

British Library Cataloguing in Publication Data
Lewery, A. J. (Anthony John), *1941*–
　Signwritten art.
　1. Signs. Lettering, history
　I. Title
　745.6′1

ISBN 0–7153–9273–5

Typeset by ABM Typographics Limited Hull
and printed in Great Britain
by Redwood Burn Limited, Trowbridge
for David & Charles Publishers plc
Brunel House　Newton Abbot　Devon

*To the memory of Barbara Jones, artist and author,
who bridged the gap between fine art and popular
art so positively.*

Acknowledgements

This book has been in the making for a very long time, and during those years many people have given me help or snippets of information which finally brought the book into being. Some people may have been forgotten, and I hope they will accept my apologies for not being included here, but I do know that my thanks are owed to all the following: John Anstee, Harry Arnold, James Ayres, John Bell, Nicholas Biddulph, Alan Brown, Frank Carline, Arnold Cook, Crosby Cook, Harold Cooke, Dave Cooper, Jim Darwen, Sid Duckworth, the late George Dutton, John Gorman, Chris Griffiths, Adrian Jarvis, Wilf Kennerley, Chris Ketchell, Janet Kraus, Andy Millward, James Mosley, Philip Pacey, Ken Sequin, the late Frank Smith, Moira Stevenson, Maurice Thake, Harry Ward and Kenneth Yates.

Both Nigel Carter and Ross Williams have given me a lot of practical photographic help for which I am grateful, and my wife Mary has typed and retyped my notes and manuscript with patience, and given encouragement.

My special thanks are due to the following signwriters who gave up their time to answer my questions: Gerry Cross, Billy Gilpin, Ray Manning, Cyril Moss and Joseph Waring, and to Robert McGoran for looking after, and also trusting me with, Mr Gee's apprentice notebooks. I do hope they all approve.

All photographs are by the author unless otherwise credited.

Contents

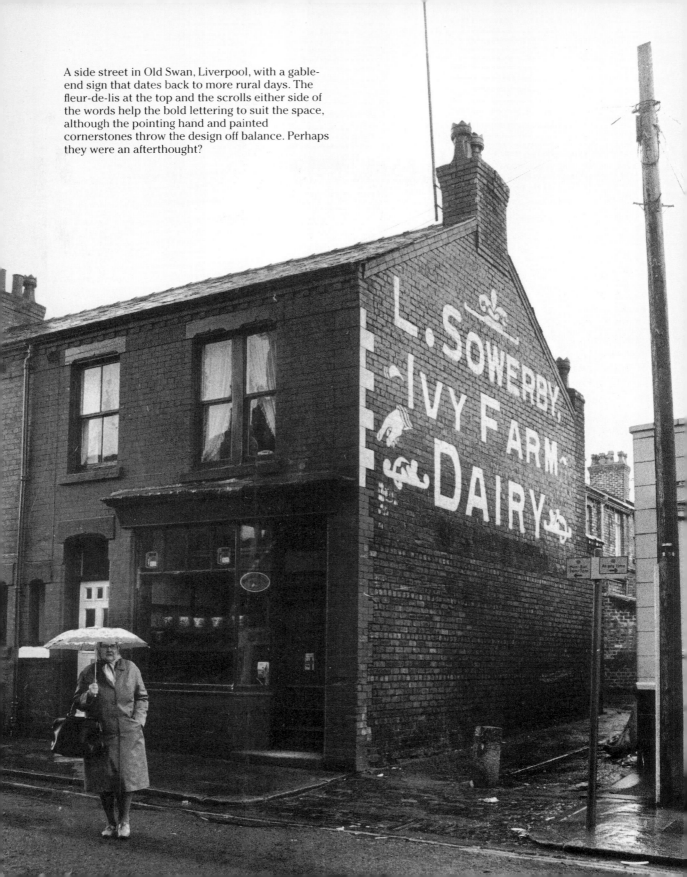

A side street in Old Swan, Liverpool, with a gable-end sign that dates back to more rural days. The fleur-de-lis at the top and the scrolls either side of the words help the bold lettering to suit the space, although the pointing hand and painted cornerstones throw the design off balance. Perhaps they were an afterthought?

⦿ INTRODUCTION ⦿

AND SOME DEFINITIONS

THIS book is about the Art of signwriting as much as the Craft, and describes the over-all visual quality of the work as well as how it was produced. There is some practical information, of course, but its prime purpose is to inspire a greater interest in a skilful and under-rated trade, one that often produces perfect examples of popular art, and sometimes creates work which can even be regarded as true folk art. Most painters' and decorators' manuals include some practical signwriting instructions, and the old books written specially for the signwriter, although sometimes difficult to find, are still quite valid today (see bibliography). This book records past and present work, for although signwriting is not as prevalent as it was even twenty years ago, it is surviving and adapting to modern conditions quite well – a continuity of tradition that reaches back for at least one hundred and fifty

A man of so many trades probably did the sign-writing too. An unexpected mixture of sophistication at the top with rustic simplicity at the bottom.

years, and perhaps much more.

Popular and folk art are awkward concepts to be precise about, and it will probably be useful to start with some discussion of these vague terms. 'Art' means many things to different people – the art of conversation, the art of the wheelwright, the art of Michelangelo and even folk art. It might help to clarify the difference between *craft* and *art*. Art results in a work of art, a creation that in turn creates a deep response in the viewer, a successful fusion between the artist's intention, the medium, and the recipient's emotional response. Craft, however, is simply the ability to handle a given material accurately and to produce an acceptable job consistently. It happens that a good craftsman will often go

beyond that and, perhaps unconsciously, produce work that meets all the requirements of a work of art as well. He is then an artist as well as a craftsman, but it would be wrong to say that another workman, who cannot reach that art standard, is not therefore a craftsman. It is equally wrong of course to assume that fine craftsmanship is necessarily good art. The quality of a poem is not altered by the way it is written down. Art is about the emotional response, craft is the practical handling of materials and techniques. Happily the two are so often involved and interdependent that this separation is quite unnecessary, but in the field of the unacademic artist – the Naive or Primitive painter or the folk artist – it helps to remember that the art does not finally depend on the technique.

The visual artist's job is to arrange colours, line, pattern and texture in such a way that it evokes an intentional emotional response, which in some tiny way changes the viewer's perception of reality towards his own. He has

---

A powerful signboard outside Ulverston in Cumbria, painted by Billy Gilpin, the locality's signwriter for over fifty years. His personal style of lettering appears throughout the area as a significant part of the local visual culture.

usually used these ingredients to arrange recognisable images of people, animals, landscape or weather to this end too, but it is not actually a prerequisite – a fact restated and explored by the abstract art movements of the twentieth century. Unfortunately this abstract development raced ahead of the ordinary art education of the majority, set in its traditional form, and further widened the gap between popular taste in pictures and 'fine' academic art as taught in art schools. However, this gulf between the unsophisticated taste of the working population and the artistic standards of the educated elite has existed for a long time, and accounts for the fact that there is a need to discuss popular art as a separate category at all. After the renaissance of the sixteenth and seventeenth centuries the aristocracy and educated elite pursued and promoted the ideals and standards of Ancient Rome for two hundred years, to the almost complete exclusion of the home-grown Gothic culture. Anything that smacked of our rude medieval past was frowned on, and the only arts that were acceptable to this powerful upper-class minority were those that revealed their classical breeding. As polite society bred and interbred, the fine arts that it patronised and encouraged came to be associated with its aspirations and standards of beauty. Good breeding required an education, and education was substantially based upon a knowledge of ancient classical art. Thus classical art and architecture became a visible symbol of good breeding and the exclusive class circle was complete.

Meanwhile the rest of the population continued to earn their bread and spend their spare time in much the same way that they always had, and from the limited evidence that survives it is assumed that the popular culture continued with little change. The development of industrialisation in Britain changed all that, however, and rather earlier and more completely than in the rest of Europe. With the growth of towns and the increasing organisation of labour by a management class, the

mass of the population changed quite rapidly from an old rural peasantry to a new urban working class, and much of the old culture ceased to be relevant, and was discarded. By the nineteenth century, the boom-time of industrial expansion, the working class came under increasing pressure from both commercialism and education to spend their time and money on art and artefacts that reflected the taste of their bosses and social betters, to emulate the educated elite and discard anything coarse or unsophisticated. In combination with the increasing tide of mass-produced goods that removed the practical need for them to make things themselves, it is small wonder that little remained to the Victorian people, or remains to us, that can be called folk or popular culture. But it does still exist, and the fact that something survives and that new things have developed proves its importance, not only to past generations but to us as well.

The words 'folk' and 'popular' are often used together and are sometimes interchangeable. Most authors of books on folklife subjects prefer not to be drawn into the deep water of tight definition; precise boundaries tend to breed experts and specialist argument, and the truth of the whole subject gets lost in trivial disagreements about details. However, there is a difference, even if the definitions sometimes merge at the edge. Popular art has simply got to be popular, to be liked by a large number of people for a long time, regardless of their education or lack of it, and this reflects some very basic human tastes. Folk art does that too, but in a purer form, and is an actual expression of unsophisticated taste, rather than a reflection. The word 'folk' means 'people', and used as an adjective it means 'of the people', the mass of them rather than a privileged few, but it is so overlaid with subtle meanings depending on surroundings and upbringing that it has many different connotations. There are written definitions of what constitutes folk art, but in endeavouring to be both accurate and inclusive we get statements

like 'folklore is whenever in many callings the knowledge, experience, wisdom, skill, the habits and practices of the past are handed down by example or spoken word by older to new generations without reference to book, print, or schoolteacher'. Though this may well be correct, it needs quite an effort to absorb that kind of statement. Another definition is 'the accumulated store of what mankind has experienced, learned and practised across the ages as popular and traditional knowledge as distinguished from scientific knowledge'. Four things seem important in deciding whether a work is truly folk art: who does it, who it is done for, the style and the purpose. They are all interdependent of course, but it is easier to describe by four simple interdependent statements, than to try to link them into one instantly forgettable sentence.

A folk artist is an ignorant artist. There is no insult intended there – it is just that his work must be sufficiently unaffected by the teaching of fine or academic art for him to be content to use traditional patterns and techniques without radical alteration, and to be willing to satisfy the demands of his customers on their own level, without trying to alter their tastes or educate them. He can certainly become very skilled at his trade in time, because if he keeps his work acceptable he will be getting a lot of practice in handling the tools, as well as in more nebulous things like colour and composition. His customers also have traditional standards of craftsmanship that they expect to be maintained, if not improved. The training, if there is any, will be from master to apprentice, or from father to son, by example and word of mouth rather than by textbook. The master-painter's job, if he is conscientious, is to ensure that the apprentice finishes his training

This church sign in Frodsham is another sample of a personal letter style that has become as recognisable as a familiar signature within a limited area. This example is by local signwriter John White.

The travelling showmen have always been good at using lettering dramatically for decorative effect as well as information. This good example on an Atkinson lorry was in Frodsham, Cheshire, in September 1983, but Silcocks fairs travel extensively all over the north-west of England.

Two 'backboards' from Brighton fishing boats, which were effectively backrests for the stern seats when these local rowing boats were briefly converted to tripper boats during the summer season. The owner's pride is evident, as is the old-fashioned skill of the local signwriter Harry Taylor who painted *Mary Jane*'s board in 1948 and *Pamela*'s in 1952. These perfect examples of signwritten folk art are now preserved with several others in the local fishermen's club.

---

able to do the job at least as well as himself, and the only certain way he knows is to make his protégé do it in exactly the same way, brushstroke for brushstroke. This in turn leads towards formalism and mannerism, restrains the young craftsman's work, and again reinforces the traditional way of working.

The second consideration is the customer – the group of people for whom this folk art caters. The word 'folk' means 'of the people', but how large must a group of people be, and with what sort of bond between them? At one extreme, if a man and his wife both like one particular piece of paintwork, this does not constitute their own folk art, it is merely a coincidence of taste; and yet it does not need the whole population of England to like English

canal boat painting for it to be a recognisable folk art. Similarly we would not expect English farm workers really to appreciate Hungarian rural folk art; clearly there must be a closer bond than just being people.

Culturally, artist and consumer need to be on a similar level, with a balanced relationship between them that rests on a similarity of background and education, so that the work of the artist or craftsman can be directly valued by the other without needing a cultural interpreter to explain it, and without false humility. If one is trading with the other from a different cultural viewpoint, the work exchanged between the two has falsehood built in, which will soon begin to show, like canal boat painters decorating trays for American tourists, or art-school potters making traditional salt pots which will only ever be used as ornaments.

When we come to the style, I think it is true to say that folk art must always be within a recognisable convention. If it were not so, the work would be the self-expression of one artist seeking an audience, and although it could become the stuff of folk art if sufficient people felt they needed it for long enough, that time factor would already ensure that it was at least halfway to being a convention. Because folk art is done for a specific group of people rather than an individual, it must be aimed at satisfying their demand in an assured way, in a time-honoured manner. To be accepted by that group of people it must appeal to some common denominator of their varied tastes, and the artist will vary the accepted formula at his peril. He will of course be trying little additions or rearrangements of the convention, and the general acceptance of some of these innovations over a period of time is the life and development of the tradition, but the innate conservatism of that group of people will make sure that nothing happens very fast. It is said that seeing a work of art should result in a new way of perceiving things, a new vision of reality. That is entirely opposite to folk traditions where the customer is asking for his old way of seeing things to be reinforced, and where communal attitudes are underlined and beliefs restated in the acceptable and conventional way.

The final test for a piece of folk art must be the reason for its existence, but this reason is very difficult to define, as it is always one subtle step beyond any obvious practical one. A canal boatman needs a jug to keep his drinking water in, but in practical terms it doesn't need to be painted at all, let alone with formalised flowers and landscape pictures. However, it always is, and needs to be for obscure but powerful reasons of tradition and self-esteem. A traditional signwriter, asked to paint a fascia board for a confectioner's shop might arrange the phrase 'Baker and Confectioner' on a double curve, with a line and simple flourish beneath to complete it. It doesn't say the words more clearly, but it says them more beautifully. Both boatman and signwriter have put in unnecessary work to make it better than it needed to be.

The purpose of the art is therefore decoration, which is subsidiary to the prime purpose of the object that it embellishes. If it were not so, if the purpose of the painting was the crea-

The polished dignity of this farm sign seems almost too good to be nailed to a telegraph pole outside the gate, and words painted on an old fertiliser sack might have convinced us of the wholesomeness of the produce just as well. Fine lettering by Mr Hutchinson none the less, although the interesting stretching of the word 'Fresh' does not quite connect with the 'Vegetables'. Near Macclesfield, Cheshire.

tion of something that was simply beautiful in any context, it would be 'fine art' in intention, however rough the result. The primitive and naive painters who have now received recognition as artists, like Grandma Moses and Beryl Cook, painted their pictures as pictures, with no additional purpose in mind. They must make their message, create their reaction in the beholder individually, anywhere, in the same way as any other fine artist's work, with no other practical reason for existence. Folk art on the other hand is part of everyday life for ordinary working people, some superfluous beauty and quality that proves that we

are human beings, neither plain animals nor plain cogs in an economic machine.

It will already be obvious that only a tiny proportion of modern signwriting work could fall within the strict category of folk art, but it is an interesting proportion and under-recorded, and I hope this book will draw some attention to it. However, if we exclude that large part of the trade that paints signs to studio designs prepared by graphic artists, a much more significant proportion of the work satisfies some of the criteria, and can certainly be called a part of popular art. In this category the customers or consumers are much the same, a fairly large unsophisticated part of the population, but it matters much less what cultural influences there have been, and doesn't matter at all who does it. Commercial success or failure quickly weeds out the unpopular elements and the passage of time soon shows

Extremely dated, but a fascinating piece of lettering design surviving on a lavatory window of Ludlow Market Hall, Shropshire. The hall was opened in 1887 and it seems possible that this is still the original. It was an interesting problem convincing the caretaker of this male author's honourable intentions too, for the photograph is taken from the inside looking out, and printed backwards!

The colour page from William Sutherland's 1860 book on signwriting with suggestions that set the standard for at least fifty years to come. Extreme Victoriana but still wonderful.

RICHARDSON & SON, COACH BUILDERS UTTOXETER

ROBERT FEARON LICENSED RETAILER OF SPIRITUOUS LIQUORS, WINES ALE, PORTER & TOBACCO

up short-lived fashions. When a decorative craft or trade becomes a traditional practice, and meets with the approval of continued popular acceptance, we have the basis of a popular art and an important reflection of the taste of the people for whom it is catering.

It is difficult for anyone to clearly distinguish what will eventually be regarded as a popular art of their own time because, depending on their education and taste, it is either an unexceptional part of everyday life or something in bad taste that lots of other people like. It needs to be accepted by a lot of people for a long time, to be recognised and given due respect, and then it suddenly gains an unnatural financial value as a collector's item and an investment. Protecting this investment probably means keeping it in unnatural surroundings, in a glass case or framed on the wall. However, examples of signwritten popular art are still in the right place and are still being produced. Signwriting is certainly not dying as a trade. It is not as evident as it used to be, covering every available space as it did from the nineteenth century to the Second World War, but it is now holding its own against neon, perspex, and screen printing, and shows no signs of disappearing. It is changing, however, as it must to survive, and many areas of the trade need to be recorded fast, before the memories fade with the old-style craftsmen. The following chapters are a start in that direction.

(Above) A small board now in the Staffordshire Folk Museum with a dignified and subtle layout of restrained lettering and a touch of filigree scroll-work, perfect for such a 'quality' trade.

(Below) A simple sign doing a legal job for *The Angel* in Kendal, Cumbria, but the ribbon outline that magically turns into a decorative scroll is a beautiful touch. It was repainted over a similar design with a different licensee's name in the past, but a long time ago, for the pub ceased trading over forty years ago. The sign too, has now vanished.

1

✦ Holy Writ to Signwriting ✦

A SHORT HISTORY OF THE BUSINESS

As a separately designated trade, signwriting has a relatively short history – it seems to have arisen to cater for an increasing need only in the nineteenth century. In his book of 1875, Ellis Davidson argues against the word, but it was obviously an accepted term in the 1850s when two books appeared with the expression 'signwriter' in the title. James Callingham in his very thorough volume on the subject in 1871 suggests that the word had been in use for a long time (although he is disappointed that it does not yet appear in his dictionary), and traces the history of the trade back to the mid-eighteenth-century signboard painters.

One of the illustrations from James Callingham's signwriting book of 1871.

Nathaniel Whittock, writing in 1827, does not use the expression, but writes of painting letters as useful for many decorative painters, skilful tradesmen like glass or heraldic painters who were in great demand at the time. He does not expect much from 'sign-painters' however, and begins by suggesting they keep their ambitions in check and their pictures simple, and that should they need to paint figures, they should copy the work of 'proper' artists published in books. He offers some basic sign-painting advice nonetheless. When discussing lettering he says 'Writing or lettering, either in gold or colour is not exactly the province of the decorative painter . . .' thereby suggesting that it is already a specialist trade, especially when he speaks of the 'writers on

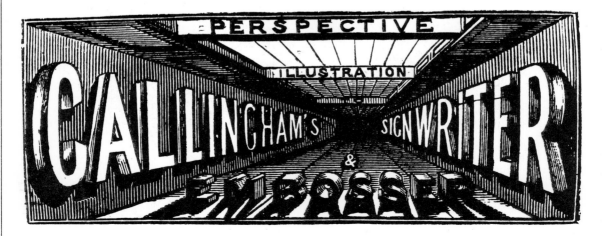

An eighteenth-century trade card from the Heal Collection in the British Museum. (Prints supplied by British Museum.)

Signpainters at work, from an early nineteenth-
century book of trades.

shop fronts, signboards, etc . . .'. His own lettering advice is rather skimpy, and based on printed rather than painted letters. Before him the evidence is very sparse, both in published material and surviving examples and we have little except the engraved trade cards of the painters and glaziers of the eighteenth century who often offer the extra services of 'Graining, Writing, Gilding &c'.

I have been unable to trace a copy of the book published in 1854 yet (see bibliography) but William Sutherland's *The Practical Guide to Sign Writing and Gilding* of 1860 seems an important landmark. He became a father figure to the decorating trade for the rest of the century through his Decorative Arts Journal publishing company. The book is large in size, but the text is short, direct and practical, with five attractive lithographed plates as illustrations. The beautifully printed colour page of large individual letters blocked up and decorated in a variety of ways may have had a significant effect on the trade throughout the country. Competitors were published in the 1870s but he answered back with new and expanded books, lavishly illustrated, in 1889 and 1898. The heights of over-elaboration and *trompe-l'oeil* paintwork were probably achieved during the 1890s, and many examples survive to the present. Little physical evidence of signwriting survives from before 1800, however, and a certain amount of guesswork is needed, although there are some pockets of information.

Church buildings provide much valuable evidence to work from. The changes brought about by the Reformation, reinforced by the Puritans, left their mark on signwriting. After centuries of increasingly rich painted decoration, the destruction by government order of images and relics marked the end of a tradition of religious wall paintings that had turned the inside of the parish church into a casket of colour, gold, and pictures, as rich as a page of medieval illuminated manuscript. Whitewash was the Puritan antidote, with the scriptural messages of the murals replaced by written

The clumsy layout and odd spelling of this stone in Hatherleigh churchyard, Devon, still suggest a lack of experience in both cutter and customer, although other letter-cutters in other parts of the country were producing immaculate well-spaced classical lettering by this date. Our modern fashion for clearing gravestones to make grass mowing easier often reveals apprenticeship practice work that should have remained decently hidden below ground, as in this example, commemorating a desperately tragic time in Robert Middleton's life.

texts and mottoes painted directly on the wall in 'church text', the formal scholars' pen lettering of the old manuscripts and the new books. These texts were probably the commonest examples of lettering on public display. A lot of this lettering still survives, and the practice continued as an important part of church decoration well into this century. Victorian antiquarianism and the Gothic revival gave it a boost, and church decoration became a speciality for some painting and decorating firms. The lettering became Victorian mock-Gothic with all the Tudor lumps and decorative holes included that the historians had rediscovered, but the principal elements remained.

The second block of lettering evidence that the church supplies is on gravestones and memorial tablets; although the medium and technique are quite different there are hints to be heeded. Outside gravestones dated before 1600 hardly exist. It may be that stone was expensive, and only slowly replaced wooden memorials, all long since rotted away, but it is probable that the humble Christian buried outside in the yard was not deemed worthy of a memorial at all. By 1700, however, they are common, and by 1800 they are standard, but the startling difference is the change in quality. Before 1650 they are generally bad in lettering terms, but by 1750 the standard has improved spectacularly. Without discussing letter-cutting history in detail, this improvement does point to an increased general awareness of public lettering and literacy, and presumably illustrates the demands and expectations of the customer, as well as hinting at changes in the standard of living and respect for the dead.

Early gravestones are a fascinating study, sometimes both tender and vigorous in design and message, and even humorous to our eyes, whether intended or not, but the lettering itself is a hotch potch, letters back to front and badly spaced, corrections and after-thoughts chiselled in anywhere, and with words spelt strangely if not wrongly. However, the expensive memorials to the rich and titled within the church are well cut and lettered and the inherited skill of the stone mason is evident in the building itself, so it is odd that the lettering outside should be quite so clumsy. It suggests an illiterate tradesman doing new business for a new class of customer, both following new fashions; a glance sideways at the expanding society of the time seems to support this idea. Reading and writing were becoming more

How odd that the craftsman capable of neatly cutting this slab in Cheshire should arrange the spacing and letters in such an ignorant way. The message itself, with its classical Roman aspirations evident in the 'V's for 'U's and 'I' for 'J', was perhaps written out by one hand and arranged by another, but why reverse the 'N's? The embarrassment of an obvious spelling mistake discovered when the job is complete is familiar to every signwriter at some time, but his mistake can usually be rectified immediately, instead of lasting for over three hundred years.

AN

EXPOSITION

ON THE

Lord's Prayer,

WITH A

Catechistical Explication

Thereof, by way of

QUESTION and ANSWER,

For the Instructing of YOUTH:

To which is added some

SERMONS

On *Providence*, and the *Excellent Advantages* of *Reading* and *Studying* the Holy *Scriptures*.

By *EZEKIEL HOPKINS*, late Lord Bishop of *London-Derry*.

LONDON:

Printed, for *Nathanael Ranew* at the *Kings-Arms*, and *Edward Mory* at the *Three Bibles* in St. *Paul's Church-Yard*, 1692.

THE

PILGRIM'S PROGRESS

FROM THIS WORLD

TO

THAT WHICH IS TO COME;

DELIVERED UNDER

The Similitude of a Dream;

WHEREIN IS DISCOVERED

THE MANNER OF HIS SETTING OUT, HIS DANGEROUS JOURNEY, AND SAFE ARRIVAL AT

THE DESIRED COUNTRY:

CONTAINING ALSO

THE PILGRIMAGE OF HIS WIFE AND CHILDREN,

AND

THEIR SAFE ARRIVAL.

BY JOHN BUNYAN,

Late Minister of the Gospel at Bedford.

IN THREE PARTS.

WITH EXPLANATORY NOTES BY W. MASON, ESQ.

AND

EVANGELICAL REFLECTIONS.

TO WHICH IS PREFIXED,

AN ORIGINAL LIFE OF THE AUTHOR.

LONDON:

PRINTED BY J. M'GOWAN AND SON,

GREAT WINDMILL STREET.

Dramatic improvements in printed lettering and layout are clear in these two examples, roughly a hundred years apart, just as gravestone cutting also improved from the seventeenth to the eighteenth centuries. Increased literacy and an awareness of good lettering went hand in hand.

---

common amongst the mass of the population, and the printed Bible was becoming more easily obtainable. However, the printed page of the seventeenth century was still rather crude in execution, with irregularities in letter shape and layout, so if it was used as a pattern by an aspiring stone cutter this might explain the rather higgledy-piggledy results.

By the eighteenth century the quality of printing had improved, and parallel improvements are obvious on gravestones. At the same time the general standard of handwriting was also improving, helped by the availability of the engraved books of the writing-masters, and this influence too can be seen on many stones. Above all else was the influence of the Renaissance, still filtering down the centuries and social classes, constantly leaning towards classical clean-cut purity and away from our crude Gothic (and Catholic) past. Roman lettering, both in its archaeological form, and as beautiful new movable type-faces developed by Italian type-founders, became the norm for printing and letter-cutting, and for any painted

Ludlow JUNE 20th 1676.

THOs. LANE Gentn. Alderman of this Corporation, gave to Twelve Poor Persons of this Town, Twelve Two Penny Loaves of Wheaten Bread to be given on every Lords Day; and for the Maintenance of that Charitable Gift for ever. Devised a parcel of Land in St. Johns

This attractive board is one of a whole clutch in Ludlow parish church in Shropshire, but the date bears no relationship to when it was done, for there are others by the same hand with various dates well into the 1820s. They are all well-preserved examples of nineteenth-century signwriting however, and many old churches are well worth visiting just to study some of the oldest examples of commercial signpainting available.

signwriting of the time. This is a much simplified genealogy of course, and there was a continuing vernacular undercurrent of popular taste. The most interesting lettering in any field is when the letter-forms combine influences and develop extra characteristics from the media in which they are worked, for then, in the best work, there is a vitality that can leapfrog both naivety of design or the boring precision of long practice. However, the influence of Rome, and the classical education of the aristocracy seeped in everywhere.

Inside the church the same fashions affect the noticeboards that detail gifts and legacies and the way they are to be used. The older the board, the more irregular the writing, more akin to pen lettering done by someone unused to a brush, than the later neatness of the professional painter. Capital letters are often of a different colour and style, reminiscent of

medieval manuscripts, but by the 1750s the mass of the lettering is in a neat lower-case roman of some sort, tight and legible two hundred years later. Some boards bearing 1700 dates may have been repainted since, but conditions in the average stone church are perfect for the long life of a painted wood panel – cool and dark, with the humidity changing very slowly from summer to winter. Many are true survivors and valuable evidence. The later and commoner boards of the nineteenth century are also interesting as examples of everyday notice writing, preserved both from the weather and from the demolition of developers. Our churches are mines of secular information as well as arks of the religious covenant.

Most old churches have some evidence of that other great influence on sign painters and writers – heraldry, known jocularly but with more than a hint of truth as the folk art of the aristocracy. Memorials dating back to the twelfth century use heraldry as both decoration and information, enriching the tomb with precious metal and colour, as well as describing the family history of the deceased to those who can read the code. It belongs firmly to the well-born and is strictly hereditary, and was at one time guarded with all the power of the law by the royal heralds, but it has become by association the popular property of all those who accept and support the aristocracy and the crown. The village church usually has some heraldic memorials to past lords of the manor and, after the Reformation, the Royal Arms were expected to be displayed as well, to reinforce the notion that the monarch was also head of the Church of England. Many of these achievements of arms, carved or painted on board or canvas are still there, dating back to the eighteenth or early nineteenth centuries – marvellous examples of the heraldic painter's art. This was often the work of a separate specialised tradesman, especially in the larger towns, and heraldic painting remained in demand throughout the nineteenth century on buildings and carriages, and for funeral 'hatchments' – memorial versions of the family arms that hung in the private chapel at church. Every painter, however humble, was expected

to understand the rudiments of heraldry, and every signwriting book still has a section on heraldry, helping to hand down an elitist privilege to the supporting populace, who can then express their national or local loyalty to a symbol.

The most common use of heraldry or elements from it is in pub names and signs, and many of the oldest, dating back to the fifteenth century, were statements of loyalty to the landowner or the crown. Red, white, and gold lions, blue boars and saracens' heads are fairly clear in their heraldic origins, but many of the more idiosyncratic names are also the result of heraldic misunderstanding or bad

Bellringing is a serious business, and although the rules of behaviour are strict, notable ringing achievements were also worthy of a signboard amongst this group in the belfry at Ashleworth, Gloucestershire. Dates range from 1881 to 1927, but the graceful rule board is possibly earlier.

Heraldic painting was still a thriving separate trade when Robert Hayward painted these Royal Arms for Knutsford church, Cheshire, in 1831, to conform with a royal edict of Henry VIII's, but he was obviously a master craftsman at letter painting as well, and proud of it. The use of the old fashioned 'f' for 's' was a bit of an affectation even then for it had long gone out of use in printing, but the panel is a beautifully dignified mixture of capitals, lower case and italic.

---

painting, like *The Bleeding Wolf* instead of a 'wolf's head erased', or *The Goose and Gridiron* for the swan and lyre, the arms of the Musicians' Company.

Alongside this legitimate heraldry, however degraded, there was the even more common-place use of jumbled and invented heraldry on tradesmen's signs, the basis of the development of the signwriters' independent trade. The expanding towns and businesses of the sixteenth and seventeenth centuries needed some sort of house identification system, and following the precedents of inns and alehouses, tradesmen advertised by hanging a sign outside; some were simple – a hat for a hatter or a knife for a cutler, but others were more subtle, using the arms of the guild or a visual pun or rebus, like two cockerels for Mr Cox's sign. The complications arose later when the business moved elsewhere, taking the trade sign to a new address, and just as heralds impaled or quartered family arms together after aristocratic marriages, so signs developed with unexpected bedfellows – the two cockerels and scissors, or the spyglass and sugar loaf. The new address was then described by its proximity to a better-known or long-established sign and we get trade cards that describe Mr Smith as residing at the 'Sign of the Leg and Seven Stars opposite The Magpie and Crown'. It was very good for the signpainters' business, if confusing for everyone else, and amongst the mass of beaut-ifully engraved trade cards and letterheads that provide us with much of our information about eighteenth-century signboards, there are many house painters and glaziers advertising themselves as sign painters, writers and gilders as well. Signwriting was not yet one word, but it was obviously becoming a specialist skill.

Several factors affected the signpainters' trade, and helped the signwriter. The proliferation of massive ornate overhanging signs got quite out of hand and after a fatal accident and several government attempts, bye-laws were passed in the 1760s directing that signs should be fixed back against the wall or taken down altogether. They were less necessary anyway as street numbering had been introduced early in the century and the great era of signboards was already in decline. Many continued in use, of course, and several trade signs and symbols are still seen today. Pubs are the most obvious, but barbers' poles, pestles and mortars for the chemist and bulls' heads for the butcher continue traditions from that period. Literacy was increasing, and when the ability to read was seen as the usual attribute of a cultured customer, so a lettered signboard suggested a better class of tradesman, especially when in the clear uncluttered style suitable to the neo-classical fashions of the Georgian and Regency periods.

The early nineteenth-century history of the trade is sketchy, with few written references to letter-painting. Whittock's 1827 book was directed to a slightly higher class of trade, and it was thirty or forty years before the publication of several books that present the trade as well-established, with a history that obviously stretched back a generation or two. Ellis Davidson in 1875 defined the job as painting 'the names, trades or other inscriptions on the architraves of shops, on show-boards (commonly called signboards) on walls, and in various other situations . . .' and he mentioned omnibuses and ships, as well as numbers on doors. In his mind it was quite separate to signpainting which dealt with images rather than words, and which was more allied to fine art than house painting. Callingham in his signwriting book of 1871 linked it with glass embossing. Advances in this related field of acid etched windows, with all the new technicalities of painting and gilding on glass, increased the scope and popularity of signwriting. It was still an expanding market and

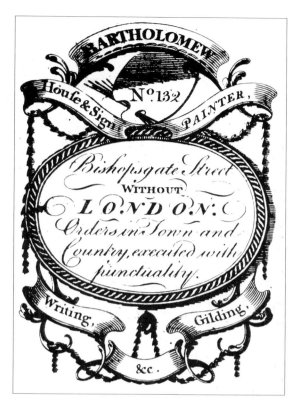

An eighteenth-century trade card from the Heal Collection in the British Museum. (Prints supplied by British Museum.)

an increasing number of books and magazines for signwriters and related trades were produced towards the end of the century. Photographic evidence increases, and many superb examples of ornate craftsmanship survive from the 1880s, although the 'art' is sometimes difficult to find under the technical brilliance of ostentatious elaboration. Like the Irish fiddler who, when asked why he played so fast replied 'because I can', so much late-Victorian design was revelling in the abilities of the expanding technologies and education of the day. The ability to deceive the eye with painted thicknesses, shadows and novelty letter-forms sometimes rendered the messages quite unreadable, but the quality of the craftsmanship was spectacularly high. This

This extravagant piece of self-advertisement from Liverpool is a wonderful catalogue of the over-elaborate lettering styles of the 1880s. It is all painted on the reverse of the glass and when photographed in the mid-1970s was in immaculate condition, a tribute to the superb craftsmanship of the late-Victorian signwriter, possibly Mr Latham himself. The frame looks kinked because this picture is made up of two photographs collaged together, necessitated by photographing it in a very small antique shop.

elaborate spectacle was in itself the imperial message at one level, however, for as rude simplicity was seen as ignorant poverty, so complex evidence of hard work and study must equate with culture and art.

In the twentieth century the design pendulum swung back again towards clarity and austerity, helped by the aftermath of two world wars, and both lettering and layout moved increasingly towards spartan simplicity and clinical purity of form. Each new sign book extolled the virtues of pure uncluttered classic roman, and muttered against the past excesses of the Victorian, although each one rather grudgingly devoted a section or so to shadowing and blocking, and decorative letter-forms. Meanwhile, out on the shopfronts and signboards of the street, traditions moved more slowly and dependable old letter-forms and decorative signwriters' tricks could still be seen despite the advent of the design pundits. This slow development was reflected in the books available, for *The Modern Signwriter*, edited by W. G. Sutherland and first published in 1923, was still the standard work and still on sale in the 1960s, and in fact much of the material in the first edition was only slightly updated from his father's *The Signwriter and Glass Embosser* of 1898. William Sutherland's influence thus spanned a century.

The first glance at most high streets today suggests that the craft of signwriting is quite dead, for so many of the shops are simply branches of multiple stores and opportunities for individual signwritten work have been drastically reduced. The economics of chain stores demand a standard house style for all their branches, projecting an image designed for the company by a design consultant, with no space for individuality at all. The brief is to prepare a master plan applicable to any shop anywhere, which in turn demands standard lettering supplied in bulk in plastic, steel or neon, or screen-printed designs using a standard typeface or a company logo. The gulf between this work and that of the old-fashioned signwriter is enormous, from a practical

Thos. Carter's shop in Chester started in business
around 1900, and we can assume that the sign dates
from the same period. It was supplied by
M. Tomlinson of Manchester, and is mainly gold leaf
lettering on glass with a black and umber shadow
on a sage green background, but touches of colour
appear on the decorated capitals and on Mr Carter's
name which is emerald green, edged with gold, dark
blue and bright red. This fine restrained sign is on
view in the Grosvenor Museum, Chester.

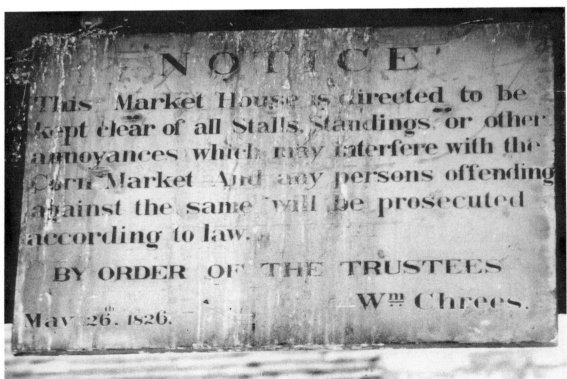

(Facing above) The young man on the right of this picture is 'B.W.K.' from Suffolk who submitted this photograph to the *Decorators and Painters* magazine in 1913. It is an attractive mixture of pictorial sign and lettering, but the use of so much acanthus leaf scroll-work is already reminiscent of the 1880s, whilst today the difficult-to-read decorated lettering would look more at home on a roundabout, rather than a milkman's shop.

(Facing below) This notice board is fixed up in the roof of the open market cross in Ledbury, in Herefordshire. It is protected from both sun and rain, and it is quite possible that this is the original signwriting of 1826. The word 'Notice' seems to be the most successful piece of lettering, but the whole thing is an amazing survival.

(Below) Some side-street signwriting in Warrington, Cheshire, by Alan Povey, a fast prolific tradesman who learnt his trade from his father Frank, and continues to work in a recognisable family style. Speed sometimes leads to odd proportions like the wide 'U' or the top-heavy 'S', but constant commercial practice also ensures a personal handwriting flow across the sign, ideal for this friendly invitation.

craftsman solving one set of signwriting problems on one particular site, perhaps working within accepted local conventions, to studio designers imposing an image on situations that they are unlikely to see, a reflection of the changed attitude to the customer. The development of the supermarket concept since the Second World War has accelerated this trend enormously. The supermarket is so successful in economic terms that smaller independent grocers have had to band together to fight back, and in order to benefit from group advertising they too have had to lose their individual styles to a corporate image.

Things are better in the back streets, although with few exceptions the signwritten shopfront is now the poor man's alternative. The only way that painting can compete with plastic is by doing it very fast and very cheaply, but to be cheap it has to do away with all the labour-intensive preparation, second coating and varnishing. Paint then becomes a tempor-

(Above) Two printers 'cuts' for use as bill heads or tailpieces from an American typefounder's catalogue of 1882.

(Facing) Watchmaker's shop in Bromyard, Worcestershire, with gilded fascia panels done by Mr Cave's own father in 1928, and in excellent condition.

ary measure, looking good for a season or so, but rapidly deteriorating to a faded shabbiness which is not a good advertisement for painter or customer. Happily there are still those that demand high-quality signwriting, and there are still areas that can only be satisfactorily lettered by hand, shapes that are awkward in outline or surface, like the unpredictable curves of vans and lorries, and jobs that need excitement and spirit in the layout, like the flamboyance of seaside and fairground. Everywhere else, pre-formed plastic and self-adhesive letters continue to make inroads.

The paragraphs above strike a rather negative note. Developments in sign technology have been spectacular, of course, and when properly carried out are a big advance in terms of permanence. The design possibilities are potentially very exciting but speed of development seems all-important, and few have invested enough time to make beautiful signs. Meanwhile the expertise and inherited arts of the old tradesman have often been ignored. Signwriting, however, does survive as a craft, with traditions and conventions like any other, and it deserves the same respect as black-smithing, chair-bodging or any of the other hand crafts that come under close scrutiny as they retreat from modern life. Signwriting is a vigorous trade adapting to new demands, and although new processes have reduced the hand-crafted part of the trade, the experience is still there to be drawn on. There is no excuse for re-inventing the trade in the mind and then making up a hypothetical history, for the men can still speak for themselves.

(Above) It does not matter what the words say on this kiosk in Morecambe, for the message is clearly of fun and holiday indulgence, expressed by the signwriter with good-humoured lettering in cheery colours.

(Below) An attractive unpretentious shopfront in Reading in proper greengrocer's colours, with traditional phrases in script flanking the proprietor's name.

2

⇒" TWO BOYS IS HALF A BOY "⇐

TRAINING FOR THE TRADE

SIGNWRITERS are an independent bunch, not exactly wild or Bohemian, as you might expect on the fringe of the art world, but just plain independent. It is a fairly solitary trade and those that make it their private business have to be able to work alone in many different situations. Some specialise, some have large well-equipped workshops, but others have nothing but a small sign kit in a box in the back of the car. Even those that work for a larger decorating firm will have their own separate sign shop at the back of the works. Here they will have time to think as well as work, and the majority of signwriters seem to have a refreshingly thoughtful and contemplative approach to life.

A few signwriters are self-taught, but many of the good ones, with a high degree of old-fashioned craftsmanship, learnt their trade through an apprenticeship of some sort, either formally by being indentured to one firm or master craftsman, or informally as a son to his father. Often the self-taught ones started in the painting trade in some other form, as ordinary house painters or decorators, and studied to get themselves out of it because up to the Second World War house painting was poorly paid and there were long periods of winter unemployment. Good money could be earned during the 'season', even at a low hourly rate, by working from dawn to dusk all spring and summer, but autumn mist and rain meant the

laying-off of most of the men from the big firms for the winter. The only ones retained were the most senior foremen, the specialist grainers or signwriters who could be found inside work to earn their keep, and the apprentices. In a beginners' book of 1879 Mr Badenoch exhorts the student to persevere for 'there is money to be made by it, yea, and there is inside work in bad weather with less heavy labour to be undergone', for one of the banes of the brush-hand's life was constantly humping heavy wooden ladders and wooden scaffolding about. With a high rate of pay and regular comfortable work in the warm, a good signwriter in a good firm was a man to be envied. His position in relation to a young apprentice was described as something 'almost celestial' by one old signwriter.

An apprentice is someone who agrees to work at a trade for a fixed period for a minimal wage, or even for nothing at all, and be thoroughly taught that trade in exchange. It used to be a much tougher legal contract than it is now, both sides being bound by an 'indentured' legal agreement between the employer and the boy's parent or guardian, the lad to work unquestioningly under the orders

---

It is easy to understand the link between signwriter and house painter, but it now seems strange that the trade was also often run with that of plumbing and gasfitting.

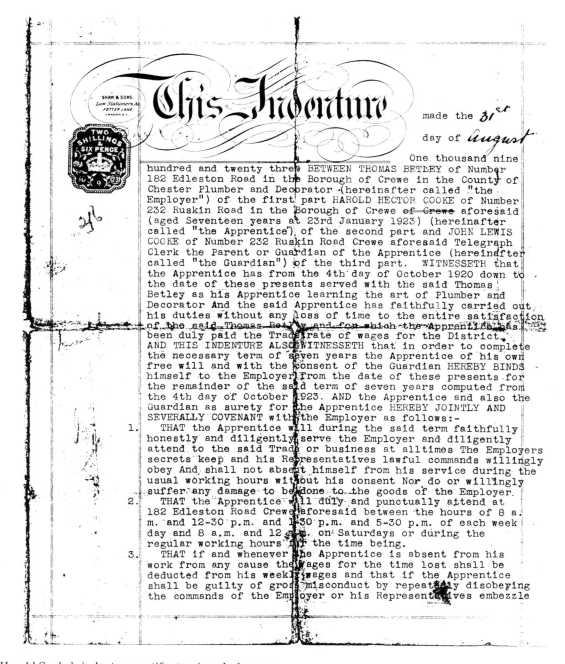

This Indenture made the 31st day of August One thousand nine hundred and twenty three BETWEEN THOMAS BETLEY of Number 182 Edleston Road in the Borough of Crewe in the County of Chester Plumber and Decorator (hereinafter called "the Employer") of the first part HAROLD HECTOR COOKE of Number 232 Ruskin Road in the Borough of Crewe of Crewe aforesaid (aged Seventeen years at 23rd January 1923) (hereinafter called "the Apprentice") of the second part and JOHN LEWIS COOKE of Number 232 Ruskin Road Crewe aforesaid Telegraph Clerk the Parent or Guardian of the Apprentice (hereinafter called "the Guardian") of the third part. WITNESSETH that the Apprentice has from the 4th day of October 1920 down to the date of these presents served with the said Thomas Betley as his Apprentice learning the art of Plumber and Decorator And the said Apprentice has faithfully carried out his duties without any loss of time to the entire satisfaction of the said Thomas Betley and for which the Apprentice has been duly paid the Trade rate of wages for the District. AND THIS INDENTURE ALSO WITNESSETH that in order to complete the necessary term of seven years the Apprentice of his own free will and with the consent of the Guardian HEREBY BINDS himself to the Employer from the date of these presents for the remainder of the said term of seven years computed from the 4th day of October 1923. AND the Apprentice and also the Guardian as surety for the Apprentice HEREBY JOINTLY AND SEVERALLY COVENANT with the Employer as follows:-

1. THAT the Apprentice will during the said term faithfully honestly and diligently serve the Employer and diligently attend to the said Trade or business at alltimes The Employers secrets keep and his Representatives lawful commands willingly obey And shall not absent himself from his service during the usual working hours without his consent Nor do or willingly suffer any damage to be done to the goods of the Employer.

2. THAT the Apprentice will duly and punctually attend at 182 Edleston Road Crewe aforesaid between the hours of 8 a.m. and 12-30 p.m. and 1-30 p.m. and 5-30 p.m. of each week day and 8 a.m. and 12 a.m. on Saturdays or during the regular working hours for the time being.

3. THAT if and whenever the Apprentice is absent from his work from any cause the wages for the time lost shall be deducted from his weekly wages and that if the Apprentice shall be guilty of gross misconduct by repeatedly disobeying the commands of the Employer or his Representatives embezzle

Harold Cooke's indenture certificate, signed when he had already been 'learning the art of Plumber and Decorator . . . without any loss of time, to the entire satisfaction' of his employer for three years in 1923. He went on to become an accomplished grainer, and a signwriter at Crewe railway works.

or make away with any of the goods or effects which may be
entrusted to his care or in case of the breach non-observance
or non-performance of any of the covenants or agreements
herein contained on the part of the Apprentice the Employer
may forthwith discharge the Apprentice and cancel this
Indenture whereupon the weekly wages shall immediately
cease and be no longer payable and this Indenture and every
covenant clause and thing herein contained shall be void
and absolutely determined.   AND in consideration of such
service the Employer hereby covenants with the Apprentice
and also with the Guardian as follows:-

1. THAT the Employer by his Manager or Assistants will
during the said term according to the best of his power
skill and knowledge teach and instruct or cause to be taught
or instructed the Apprentice.

2. THAT the Employer will pay to the Apprentice during
the said term during such time as he shall be able to and
actually perform his service weekly and every week:-

During the 4th year of Apprenticeship, 18/3   per week
    "   "   5th   "   "   One   "   Pound   "   "   "
    "   "   6th   "   "   "   £1-3-0   "   "   "
    "   "   7th   "   "   "   £1-8-0   "   "   "

IN WITNESS whereof the said parties to these presents
have hereunto set their hands and seals the day and year
first above written.

SIGNED SEALED AND DELIVERED by   )
the before named Thomas Betley   )
Harold Hector Cooke and John   )
Lewis Cooke in the presence of:-)
)

H. Lockwood
11 Laston Street
Crewe
Clerk.

Thomas Betley

Harold H Cooke

John Lewis Cooke

of the master-craftsman whilst the master agreed to teach, feed, clothe, and sometimes house the boy as well. It was a hard practical system, a hang-over in some ways from the medieval trade protection practices of the guilds, but still satisfactory enough for parents in Victorian, and even Edwardian times to pay the master-craftsman a considerable sum of money, the apprenticeship 'premium', to ensure their sons had a proper schooling to a good trade. It was a system built on trust, the boy to work and the man to teach, but the power of the master left it open to abuse, and with the increasing pressure of nineteenth-century business competition the lad was often used as cheap labour in exchange for very skimpy teaching.

Liberal-minded Victorians recognised this, and by the turn of the century more government influence was seeking to protect the apprentice. The period from the time he started work at twelve or thirteen years old to becoming a full vote-carrying adult at twenty-one was increasingly seen as a time for further education, both within his chosen trade and in the general subjects of elementary education, and more and more evening classes were made available, and finally made compulsory. In 1913 the Education Act insisted that boys should be allowed to go to classes for one day a week, in the firm's time and at the firm's cost. Another blow to the old-fashioned apprentice-ship system was dealt by the First World War, when the whole new generation of older apprentices returning from the trenches could no longer be treated as ignorant boys, and the value of their labour was recognised by a rise in wage levels. They started very low for the fourteen-year-old but rose year by year through the seven years of a standard apprenticeship until, as he 'came out of his time' and became a journeyman craftsman, they equalled the locally negotiated rate for a full tradesman. Even then some firms only paid an improver's rate, still well below that of a tradesman.

In the 1920s and the 1930s the painting and decorating tradesman's rate was around 1/6d to 1/9d an hour (approximately 7½ to 8p), a weekly wage of between £3/10/- (£3.50p) to £4.00, although this could be much higher in the summer with overtime. An apprentice would get about 8/- a week (40p) until he was fifteen years old when it would start rising by increasing amounts each year so that his wages were an increasing proportion of the full tradesman's rate, for example, one ninth the first year, one seventh the second, one sixth the third, and one quarter the fourth. Rates of pay varied a little around the country, but remained stable for very long periods. A good painter and decorator was earning 6d to 7½d (2½p to 3p) an hour back in the 1880s and the rate had only risen to 2/6d (12½p) at the end of the Second World War sixty years later. It was the escalation and inflation of the 1960s and 1970s that now makes these figures look so ridiculous and difficult to compare. But the signwriter was always a high-grade tradesman and able to make considerably more than that if he practised enough to become fast, and also branched out on his own. As William Sutherland said in 1860, 'any man having a good practical knowledge of Sign Writing may get a good living in almost any part of the civilised world'. In a 1928 book on estimating for decorators' work the author says that 'the average earning power of a writer is double that of a house painter . . .' and adds ruefully that as all signwriters seem to quote 3d per inch for signwriting and get a very good living, he is sure that writing can be done for one penny an inch if necessary.

It was exceptional for a fourteen-year-old to be aiming to become, or apprenticed as, a signwriter directly, for it was regarded as a speciality within a broader trade, and most lads this century were apprenticed as 'Painter, Decorator, Signwriter and Grainer', or perhaps as 'Coachpainter', a very high class trade that expects its men to be good at lettering and lin-ing as well. Their ancestors were the carriage-makers and heraldic painters of the aristoc-racy, and some still see their trade as a cut above the common house painter, even

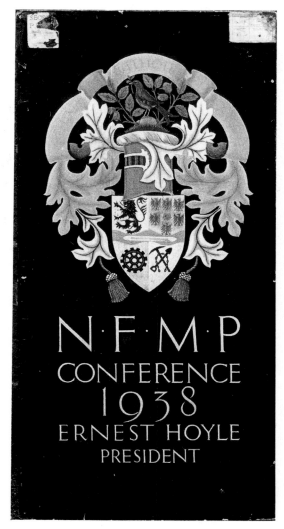

N·F·M·P
CONFERENCE
1938
ERNEST HOYLE
PRESIDENT

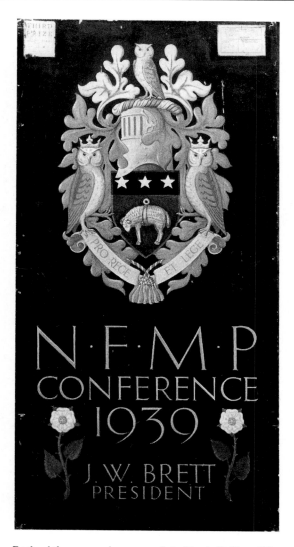

N·F·M·P
CONFERENCE
1939
J. W. BRETT
PRESIDENT

though their high standards are now applied to run-of-the-mill lorries and coaches. The house painter is really a specialist of the building trade; many of the old engraved business cards linked the painter and glazier together, with plumbing increasingly involved as the nineteenth century progressed – all being linked by their use of putty and lead. The decorator crept in as more of an artist, painting designs on ceilings and walls, cutting stencils and gilding cornices and mouldings, but his trade gradually merged with that of the house painter as tastes changed, costs went up and

Both of these panels were painted by L. F. Meredith of Leamington Spa as apprenticeship competition pieces, and show a very high standard of both art and craftsmanship. Perhaps they were judged by the president of the National Federation of Master Painters at the conference, but he only awarded Mr Meredith second prize in 1938 and third in 1939.

cheaper wallpapers took over the patterning of walls from hand-craftsmanship. Elements of all these trades remained in the apprentices' evening classes however, even into the 1960s, where training was still offered in free-hand drawing and painted design, as well as lettering and graining. The breadth of this general art education gave a keen lad the chance to discover his own natural talent, and in a large decorating firm a taste for lettering and fine work would soon be noticed by his foreman or boss, who would increasingly put him to work with the specialist signwriter.

There were always a number of specialist sign firms taking on lads as signwriting apprentices only, and there has always been the self-employed man teaching his son, but they all face the same problem of teaching the trade. Good signwriting depends on fluency with the brush and constant practice, and the only way to learn is to do it. The problem is to find work for the beginner that will give him that practice, whilst still paying his way. A philanthropic boss could find some time for the lad to practice on paper or on boards that could be wiped clean again, and the evening or daytime classes were helpful, but the boy wasn't earning his living however small the wage. The favourite way was to start the apprentice second-coating lettering that had already been laid out and undercoated by a tradesman, or filling in lettering that had already been outlined. A regular apprenticeship job for one of my informants was to paint the title of the week's film on the white glass

dropper of the cinema's queue canopy. It only had to last a week and was written up in an easily removable flat paint, whilst the lad was 'watched by all the out-of-works on the other pavement, audibly spelling it out, wondering what it would say'. This sounds like nerve-racking training for a theatrical career as well as for signwriting.

It was unusual in the larger firms for a boy to be strictly apprenticed to one man, for it made more sense to share the trouble of an ignorant youth amongst several men, as well as offering him their combined experience to learn from. It was only later as his skill became more valuable or more specialised that he was likely to work with the master-craftsman alone. In a union shop there could only be one apprentice for every four men anyway, for they were concerned to keep their members in fully paid work instead of having the trade flooded with newcomers, or alternatively having the work done by the cheap labour of apprentices. It was an unscrupulous practice that certainly happened in hard times at the rough end of the painting trade, where partially trained lads did painters' work at low wages, and then got the sack when they reached twenty-one as they were too expensive to employ. The reverse of this coin was the conscientious employer who spent time and effort teaching a lad the trade, only to have him poached by another firm when he had become useful and profitable. The indentures of a proper apprenticeship protected the original employer, for without that guarantee that he had completed his training properly, the part-trained tradesman would find it difficult to get another job later on.

The compulsory evening classes ensured that the lads got a general trade education regardless of the firm's speciality or the meanness of the boss, for they covered a broad field, although often rather outdated. Apart from the general classes in basic mathematics and English, which were compulsory until eighteen, they covered the theoretical approach as well as the practical, the chemistry of paints and

An evening class of painting and decorating apprentices at work at the Laird School of Art, Birkenhead, in about 1955. In the first picture the proportions and subtleties of the Trajan roman alphabet are being committed to paper, whilst the lads in the second photo practise block lettering. Most technical colleges offered similar courses then, but most were discontinued in the 1960s and early 1970s, and the resurgence of interest in the mid-1980s found only a very few colleges able to offer instruction courses. (Both photographs from the Frank Carline Collection.)

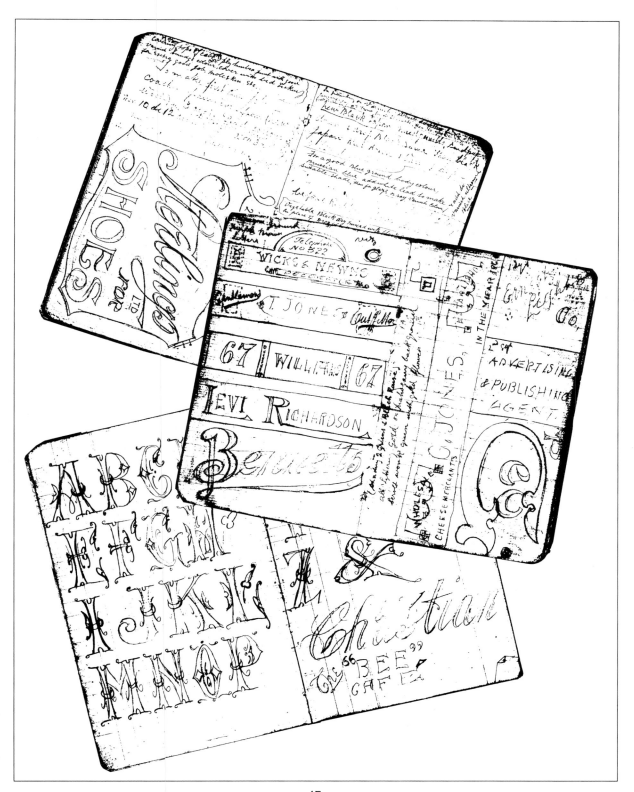

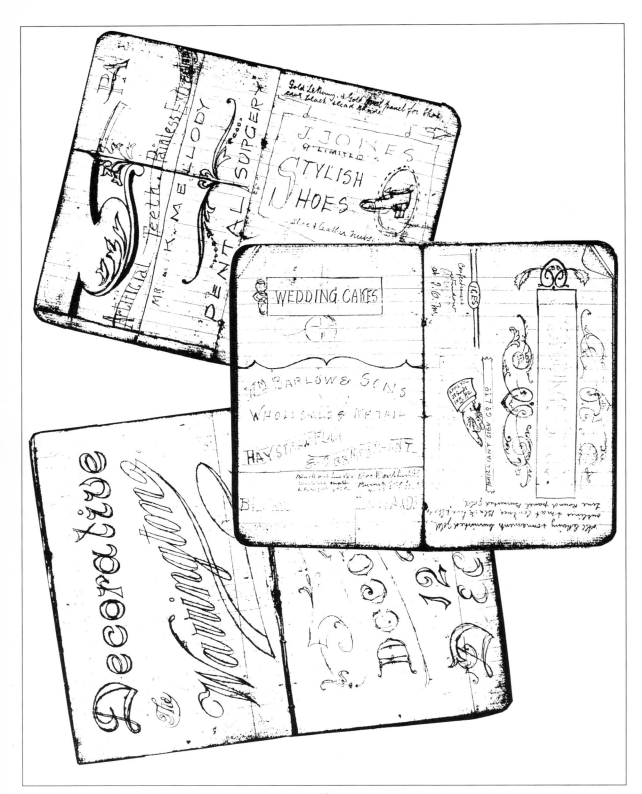

Pages from the pocket notebooks of Stan Gee, a master signwriter from Warrington, dating from around 1920 when he had just started out in business. Sketches of interesting alphabets and layouts, cuttings from magazines, working drawings and recipes for particular paints for particular jobs are all interspersed with his own costings and accounts – a mine of information.

ESTAB^D 1866

EDWARD COX

COACH BUILDER

SONNING.

First & Second Prizes at the Reading Exhibition
For Excellency of Workmanship.

SPECIALITY

The Rubber Cushioned Axle.

This beautiful signboard, now in the Reading Museum of English Rural Life, is an eloquent advertisement for the quality of Mr Cox's work as well as a catalogue of the favourite signwriters' lettering styles of the late nineteenth century. The arms at the top are the guild arms of the Worshipful Company of Coach Makers and Harness Makers, but the king is more of a puzzle. (Photograph from Museum of English Rural Life, University of Reading.)

oils, as well as how to put it on and rub it off. Panels had to be stripped down to bare wood and then brought up to a high-class finish with many coats of paint, and the exams required these panels to be finished in artificial wood-graining, or marbling, or lettered with an alphabet or two. Lessons in art and design were part of the course too: freehand drawing from life, copies from classical drawings, and styles of ornamentation from ancient to modern. Heraldry was always touched on, and a final exam piece for the practical section, produced over a couple of months of evening classes, might well be a heraldic sign design with some lettering incorporated in it. From day to day the student – particularly the student signwriter – was encouraged to keep a notebook with him at all times, to sketch signs that he liked, lettering styles or layouts, and to note down recipes of paints for special jobs. Some apprentices used them as scrapbooks as well, with examples of alphabets or scrolls culled from magazines stored away for future use, and surviving notebooks give a valuable visual record of their time as well as offering a mass of straightforward painterly information. It was a habit some tradesmen carried on with in later life, sometimes also recording the jobs done and the prices charged, making an interesting historical record.

The Second World War gave another jolt to the apprenticeship system. The more socialist post-war approach favoured more money for apprentices and less exploitation; the school leaving age was raised to fifteen and sixteen and apprenticeships were shortened so that a lad still came out of his time after his twentieth birthday but before his twenty-first. Fashions in house decoration simplified still further, and improvements in materials, making them much easier to use successfully, encouraged the untrained decorator and the 'do-it-yourself' movement. The old-fashioned painting and decorating trade has contracted considerably as a result. It followed that there was less call for formal teaching, and signwriting classes as one of the painting and decorating options virtually disappeared during the 1970s. The demands for a reasonable starting wage even for sixteen-year-olds has meant that management have had to look for more cost-effective ways of using their labour, using more machinery and less labour-intensive techniques, and any teaching is in school or on training courses, quite separate to the work place. Old-fashioned apprenticeships are virtually dead, but full-time concentrated training courses in signwriting have developed in some places instead, with some very positive

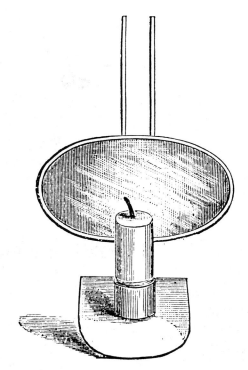

This little diagram in a 1914 handbook is a poignant reminder of long hours and old-fashioned working conditions.

aspects. Students are rather older than they used to be, have made their own choice to be there, and are thus far more committed and ready to learn. Another bonus is that the trade is at long last opening up to women, for without any excuse of needing the extra physical male strength, signwriting has always remained male-dominated.

It is difficult to make a generalised judgement on the old apprenticeship system for it was very good at one end and very bad at the other. It could be a thorough practical grounding in the trade, or exploitation of a poorly paid youth, leaving him with little to show for it. The aspect that tends to get ignored in these late school-leaving times is the more general educational value built into the system, where a lad went through adolescence and early manhood in the daily company of older men.

Today all the rebellion, which then was soaked up by long hours of labour, has to be fielded by the schoolteacher trying to cope with thirty at a time, all of whom are encouraging each other to bend the rules still further. Youth has always been awkward, and the value of young apprentices is remembered in the workman's saying, 'one boy's a boy, two boys is half a boy, but three boys is no b . . . boys at all'.

It is also difficult to judge how much the old formal part-time art lessons influenced the taste of the young signwriter. Probably the day-to-day workshop experience and the men he was working with were more important in the formation of artistic taste and signwriting practice than was theoretical teaching. Classes instilled respect for certain academically sanctioned letter-forms, but it is much easier for a young man to learn by direct experience than by theory. Second-coating a good trades-man's own style of letter quickly overtakes hours of classroom drawing work as an influence. The conscientious master-craftsman taught an apprentice in the best way he knew how – by making him do it precisely his way both in style and technique, never mind what

the book learning said, and by twenty-one the young man had absorbed a style that would probably stay with him for the rest of his working life, for better or worse.

It is this continuity that makes so much provincial signwriting particularly interesting from the popular-art point of view, for it is often out of date by fashionable standards. Tough competition in a big town pushes a competitive writer either right up to date or into severe cost-cutting and time saving, and leaves little room for frills or old-fashioned craftsmanship, but the country signwriter can indulge himself a little more. His work is sometimes a major part of the art or craft seen over a wide area, and his influence can be considerable. A correspondent to the *Journal of Decorative Art* back in 1886 compliments the magazine for its educational articles, 'for in country districts it often falls to the lot of the painter to be the sole local exponent of the beautiful in art, in form, and in colour'. This would be a bit of an overstatement today, but nevertheless signwritten lettering is still part of popular culture, and is both undervalued and unrecorded.

This imperial fascia in Liverpool, with the words arched over a painting of the British bulldog was gilded some time around the turn of the century, judging by the design, and was smashed by vandals in 1987. The shop has since closed.

CUTLERY STORES
TRADE MARK
HORNBY F. LOWE.
TABLE AND KITCHEN CUTLERY
LAWN MOWERS AND SPARES
AND GARDEN TOOLS
SCISSORS & PENKNIVES
HAIRCLIPPERS · NAIL NIPPERS
HORNBY F. LOWE.
CUTLER.
STOCKED HERE

2|0 G. PELARI. 2|0

HIGH CLASS CONFECTIONERY

ICES

3

·THE LETTERING·

ANCIENT ROME TO BLACKPOOL PIER

THE main concern of this book is the creative art of the signwriter rather than his technical ability to paint immaculate letters, even though that sort of craftsmanship must always be part of the trade. It is the personal choice of lettering and layout that is exciting, combined with its suitability for the job and its suitability for paint and brushes, especially answers worked out and tested by previous generations of tradesmen, which can be re-interpreted to satisfy modern demands. Increasingly a modern signwriter's daily work is simply enlarging and painting layouts and logos designed by someone else – someone who probably works at a studio drawingboard in an entirely different medium and scale – and it is evident in the majority of signwritten work. Unsuitable or boring letter-forms are used, that were developed as printing type or as dry transfer lettering for graphic artists and printed advertising, and true signwritten lettering is becoming increasingly rare. Since the invention of transfer lettering like Letraset or Letter Press, it is much easier for the amateur to design a neat-looking layout, whether that amateur is the boss or the secretary, and fewer artistic decisions are left to the signwriter. At the other end of the scale, the business of advertising agencies is to promote company images and all individuality needs to be sacrificed to that end. Signboards, vehicle liveries, letter-forms and logos must all conform precisely to the designer's specification for the system to work and for the advertising man to stay in business; thus any artistic interpretation by the signwriter is unnecessary. The field left for him to make any real contribution to the handmade art of the trade becomes steadily narrower. There are, however, traditional skills still being used by creative signmakers around the country, and with thoughtful use and development there will always be a demand for this smaller scale creative work, a modern use for time honoured techniques. This chapter describes some of the raw materials of the trade, the basic letter-forms that make up part of the signwriters' artistic stock in trade.

The backbone of the signwriters' lettering is roman lettering, using the term in its loosest sense – letters with a distinct contrast of thickness between vertical strokes and horizontals, and with each stroke terminated by a sharp bracketed serif. There are a huge number of variations, but they are nearly all elaborations or simplifications of the standard 'English' form of the roman letter that emerged during the eighteenth century and which has remained the most readily accepted form for

Mr Pelari's shop in Walsall, Staffordshire, with his ice-cream factory behind it, was erected in 1920 and the beautiful gilded and painted fascia was added very soon afterwards. The signwriter has invented a very distinguished expanded roman letter to fill the space, neat and crisp with a delicate dropped shadow to set it off.

A restrained statement of educational excellence, expressed in white classical roman lettering on a black school noticeboard in Liverpool.

respectable public work ever since.

The reasons for this popularity can be broadly divided into historic ones and aesthetic ones – the history of its introduction and development, and the visual quality that it possesses. Historically, the Romans themselves may have been the first people to introduce the writing into the British Isles, and four hundred years of Roman occupation left a tremendous legacy of arts and architecture, including carved inscriptions, for hundreds of years after that. However, that probably had far less influence on lettering styles than the Renaissance rediscovery of Ancient Rome a thousand years later, and the classical revivals of the eighteenth and nineteenth centuries

reinforced that influence with all the force of academically sanctioned 'good taste'. Probably more influential still was the development of printing and typography, again reflecting the Renaissance by its choice of the classical style, even to the extent of stylistically altering the manuscript-based lower-case letter into a form that suited the upper-case letters, based on carved inscriptions. This hybrid is the base for our present-day lower-case lettering.

The precise incised form of roman lettering that has survived from the classical period must have developed from an earlier style of writing, and it is usually assumed that it was pen lettering that produced the characteristic thick and thin strokes. A square-cut pen working down the page will produce a broader stroke vertically than horizontally, and a right-handed scribe will write a capital V or A with the thick strokes running diagonally down

CLASSICAL MODERN SIGNWRITER

Roman lettering through the ages from the original at the top, through the nineteenth-century 'Modern' version, to the exaggerated curves and serifs of a modern commercial writer.

---

from left to right, as in the classical inscriptions. However, the horizontal serifs and many subtleties in the letter-forms, like the slight curving in of the sides of the main strokes and on the ends of the seriffed strokes, make brush lettering the more likely ancestor. A square-ended signwriting brush can do all the work of a pen on a larger scale, and on a vertical surface. There is rare freedom of movement working with the wrist clear of the surface, and the brush can be twisted and manipulated between the fingers to make any delicate changes of stress and direction. A few surviving wall painted inscriptions in Pompeii support this idea and suggest that the modern signwriter has some very respectable antecedents, even if there was a gap of a thousand years.

The visual quality that roman-based lettering has, quite separate to lettering in general, is the vertical stress that the heavier down strokes give to a line of letters, in harmonious opposition to the lighter but definite horizontal direction that is clearly accentuated by the serifs. It is a tiny expression of the eternal argument of architecture with gravity, of the spire with the horizon and, on a philosophical level, of aspirations with our base nature.

A lot has been written about the inscription on Trajan's Column which is a fine piece of letter cutting and an important landmark in the study of our present lettering, both as a craft and an aesthetic science. It was erected in Rome in AD 114 and is thus very important as a virtually complete example of lettering design and composition from the classic period. Its importance may have been kept artificially high in Britain because there is a cast of it in the Victoria and Albert Museum, and a plea for its greatness could be read as a plea for the greatness of British museums. Every book of lettering recommends this classic example as the ideal, and a huge amount of effort has been spent measuring and copying its elegant subtleties. From the First World War to the 1960s, Trajan roman was the antidote to over-elaborated Victorian signwriting and became 'de rigueur' for any job demanding up-to-date dignity – from dustcarts and cemeteries to private boarding schools. Its main point of interest now is as the standard from which practising signwriters have deviated, the root stock from which everyday working craftsmen developed their own version of classic roman, most of which are more use and are more pleasing to the contemporary eye than the spidery elegance of a second-century memorial. Exaggerations of what started as subtle characteristics, and the alterations that creep in by everyday usage, result in individual letter styles that are not only sometimes better suited to the medium of brush and paint, but can become a recognisable personal hand-writing.

Examples of this exaggeration are usually most noticeable in the way the serifs are painted, which are quite small in the classical form, only swelling outwards about half the width of a thick stroke. There is a slight 'dishing-in' of the ends of the strokes between

the serif on either side, and the curve that brackets the point of the serif to the stem is irregular, curving sharply from the point, but more gradually as it runs into the main stroke direction. All these subtleties, pointed out to the apprentice by the night-school teacher, were never forgotten but reappeared larger than life much later, his serifs sweeping emphatically out from the main stem to end in long hair lines of cupid's bow waviness.

To counteract the optical illusion that the centres of a pair of parallel lines appear further apart than their ends, the sides of the straight strokes of the classic letter are minimally concave to avoid any optical 'thickening' in the middle. Although this is barely discernible without the aid of a straight edge, the student signwriter soon learns to use this trick to add elegance to his letters, and every straight stroke becomes a slight curve. It is actually easier to paint a satisfactory concave line than a straight one, because the human eye finds a slight deviation or wobble on a curve less noticeable than a similar fault on what was ob-

---

Chunky block lettering in gold leaf on glass, given a touch of dash with 'High Class' in italic, photographed in 1986 in Reed's bookshop just around the corner from its original address. *The Times* of 1898 is stuck firmly to the back, and there seems no reason to disbelieve that that is roughly the date of this pleasant forthright sign.

BLOCK

GROTESQUE?

SANS·SERIF

BY

SIGNWRITER

·IN·MEMORIAM·

viously intended to be a straight line. Therefore, in the absence of any direct instruction otherwise, a writer will often choose a concave-sided letter in preference to a straight one, and produce a more satisfactory job for the customer with less effort. There is also the tendency when painting any roman-based letter, to exaggerate that slight dishing of the main strokes from a masterly subtlety to an obvious stylistic trick.

The other main characteristic of roman lettering is the stress, the difference between the

The simplest measured block letters often take on some of the ancestral roman characteristics of stress and serif when they are done with the signwriter's brush.

———

thick and thin strokes, and the proportion of their thickness to the height. This can vary a great deal, changing the nature of a block of lettering quite radically in both atmosphere and pattern. The classical Trajan letters have thick strokes about one-eleventh of their height, with the thin strokes roughly half that

Sans-serif lettering thoughtfully used on an awkwardly shaped board for a side entry in Leominster, Hereford. Both layout and lettering gently 'date' it, but how much better it looks than the screw-on Egyptian letters of the same vintage on the fascia. Painted by a Mr Blundell about 1957.

---

width. The effect is elegant but rather colourless, and the early typefounders increased the contrast and reduced the relative height a little. In the eighteenth century the contrast was increased still further, and the serifs were reduced to simple hair lines of the same thickness as the thin strokes – a letter-form that is now still called, confusingly, a 'modern' face. Painted examples of this style survive on noticeboards in many churches, and suggest that the signwriter was using it long before it appeared in printed form in the 1780s.

The nineteenth century saw every possible variation tried out in print and paint, but the thickness of the standard signwriters' roman alphabet, as recommended by Callingham's book in 1878, was one fifth of its height, and that remains a good practical and legible proportion to the present day. The Victorian hair line thin strokes have given way to something more robust, about a quarter to a third of the main stroke, but in other respects the signwritten form has changed little in one hundred years, and has no need to. It still speaks clearly, regardless of fashion.

By far the commonest letter-form in signwriting work today is the simple capital block letter, the basic unadorned shape without serif, stress or fuss. It is easy to do, and is fast and cheap, but its main and dubious advantage is the rather negative value of not having any insistent mood of its own. It is not, therefore, strikingly *un*suitable for almost any job, and its use needs little aesthetic judgement to satisfy an undemanding customer. The main impact now is as a firmly twentieth-century letter, although it made its first signwritten appearance back in 1750, according to Callingham. The first 'sans-serif' typeface, without any serifs or contrast of thick and thin, was invented in the early nineteenth century as a display face, but so odd did it appear then that later versions were named 'grotesque', a name that has stuck as a generic term for this style in the printing trade. This description seems unsuitable to the twentieth-century mind, simply because this letterstyle appears so very normal and basic, the rootstock from which more complicated variations would grow. In fact, the reverse was true.

After the First World War, Edward Johnson designed a new sans-serif alphabet for the London Underground, and this, along with Eric Gill's typographic version of ten years later, became a very fashionable and potent image for the new streamlined century and remained so for the following fifty years. Johnson's lettering was built on a proportion of one to eight, the thickness of the letter being one eighth of its height, but Gill's sans-serif was slimmer and echoed the Romans by being in a proportion of one to ten. Later fashions have designed extremely skinny letters as a metaphor for elegance, but in general the signwriter favours something more meaty and reliable. One to six or seven is about average, but by making the horizontals thinner than the verticals and re-introducing the roman contrast, the main strokes can be increased to a quarter or a third of the height, and a very fat-faced message comes across. Cheery versions of this are to be seen in every holiday resort.

A combination of a more normally proportioned sans-serif letter with roman-style definition between thick and thin strokes is an attractive and useful hybrid, and extremely legible. If the sides of the letter strokes are dished a little, the resulting swelling towards the end gives a hint of serif without being conventionally historic, and is the style that could be called 'signwriters' sans-serif'. A slim version, openly spaced, reads as a high-quality modern letter, but it can be expanded or condensed, made heavier or lighter, or pushed over into an italic; in any form it always has the humanity of being hand-painted, and is fast. If the concave sides are made even more extreme so that the stems have hardly any width at the centre, but end in a sharp triangle at top and bottom, with the curved letters re-designed to suit, the result is a Gothic spikiness very popular in the 1880s, which is almost unreadable. Many examples can be found in church windows and memorials of the period, showing the battle between legibility and fashionable decorative overkill.

Another letter-style invented by the signwriter and later adapted by printers is 'Egyptian', which the Americans perversely call 'Block'. Its chief characteristic is the use of square-

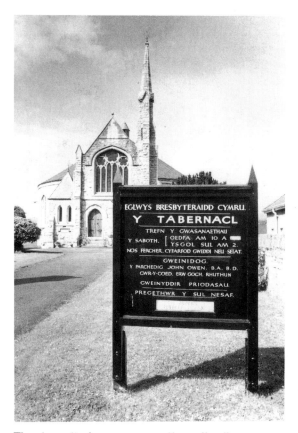

The signwriter's own sans-serif usually allows some contrast between thick and thin strokes to creep back and dishes the sides of the main strokes a little. In this example from Ruthin in North Wales the first line has a lot of comfortable contrast, whilst 'Y Tabernacl' is much more serious with an equal thickness throughout. A distinguished sign for a sober job.

This heavyweight Victorian display face still finds favour for decorative work especially when blocked out and shaded.

EGYPTIAN

It can surely be no accident that the signwriter chose a Clarendon letter style for the company name on this lorry cab, seen here on an M6 lorry park. It is painted in cream and blocked out with red on a deep maroon cab, all neatly coachlined in red and cream, a very smart example of a traditional approach to a modern truck.

---

ended slab serifs, which are sometimes as thick as the main strokes. The introduction of this heavyweight letter coincided with the early nineteenth-century interest in Egyptian antiquities and architecture, which presumably suggested the name, although it might more accurately be called 'Neolithic'. The thickness and weight can vary according to taste, as can the thickness contrast, but the serifs are generally the same width as the thin strokes. When the whole letter is fairly slim and without contrast it has a pleasant worka-

day crispness and suits modern work very well, especially with an outline, but a heavy contrast looks much more old-fashioned, and particularly suits traditional-style work, with all the traditional paraphernalia of raising and shading. If the square-ended serifs are bracketed, that is, if they are joined to the main strokes by a curve instead of a corner, the general style is called 'Clarendon' or 'Ionic'; if the ends of the serifs are then angled outwards, we arrive at 'Footed Roman', a very satisfactory, although rather dated, signwritten letter that is still to be seen on more traditional shop fascias. It has the weight of security – a touch of class from its roman ancestor with a little humour in the serifs – a valuable letter.

It is possible that the origin of the Ancient Roman serif was in the use of a paint brush – it was the lead-in to a stronger brush mark, the point where the brush first touched the surface before swelling out under the full pressure and movement of the downward stroke. It is certainly the way the signwriter now copies the carved letters, starting at the serif point and painting down the side of the letter stroke in one movement from top to bottom, finishing by lifting the brush off as it swings out into the foot serif. He then paints the other side similarly, and fills in and straightens the top and bottom, but if the ends are left untouched, the serifs appear as sprouting leaves and the split ends give a line of lettering a very decorative texture. When this is formalised, with strongly concave sides and the horizontal bars finished off with scrolled leaf growth, it is known as 'Tuscan' after the most primitive of the ancient orders of architecture. It is very pretty lettering, and was much in favour in the Edwardian period, the time of decorative music covers and cast-iron seats masquerading as wood. With extra blobs or growths sprouting from the

---

(Right) Tuscan is the most exuberantly decorative letter-form of all, and is still a fairground favourite. Upper examples are from music covers and the lower ones are from a Victorian type catalogue.

ANDANTE
POPULAR
FIRST SONATA
SONG & CHORUS.
TUSCAN
VARIATIONS ON·A·THEME

SHEPHERDS' CROOKS ENTERTAINING

ORNAMENTAL SEED-DROPPING

PRETTY DAMSEL SUN-TIPPING

CHERUBIC WITCHES MISREPRESENTATION

ORNATE ALPHABET HEREFORDSHIRE

WHIRLIGIGS AND WEATHERCOCKS

WHORTLEBERRY

The Edwardian feel of this Tuscan lettering suits its job and its riverside site in Llangollen, Clwyd, very well, and the double cross-strokes add a very attractive distinction – friendly but firm. One wonders if the houses vary in style as much as the letters suggest – morning coffee at Lauriston, afternoon tea at Braddan, and a wild party in the evening at The Mount.

---

centre line it is the basis of many more decorative and romantic styles, reaching its ultimate potential as part of the baroque extravagance of the fairground. It does not need to be that complex, however, and a simple version can be done very fast. It still recurs on quick friendly notices everywhere, rural simplicity with a touch of nostalgia.

The majority of traditional signwriters' work requires capital letters much more than lower-case letters, although graphic designers have made greater use of them in fashionable work since the 1950s. Their main use is on noticeboards with longer blocks of text, conveying information rather than advertising, and these generally follow the example of the printed page and use a painted version of a printed letter. One of the other two commonest ways of painting small letters is 'Olde English' style, or one of the many varieties of script; but if legibility is of prime importance, roman is regarded as the best, considering all the practice that the public has reading books and newspapers. This miniscule lower-case alphabet started from the same Ancient Greek and Roman markings as did the capitals, but has changed considerably as it came to us through a thousand years of scholarly hand-writing. It was the handwritten books and illuminated manuscripts of the church that the early typefounders took as their models,

Ellesmere Port Gas Works.

INCHES 1 2 3 4 5 6 7 8

developing movable typefaces of the sharp-angled 'Blackletter' style, and the italic and roman lower case rounder cursive hand of the Venetian scholars. This was re-designed as the Renaissance progressed, to complement the classical roman capitals which were regarded as the ultimate standard of educated excellence, and the metamorphosis was complete. Typefaces designed in the sixteenth and seventeenth centuries are still used, and still read clearly.

The signwritten version of these letters, like the upper case, tends to exaggerate the subtleties, and the contrast between thick and thin strokes can be extreme, from heavy to hair line, clearly reminiscent of the square-cut pen strokes. Serifs might be angled or horizontal, bracketed with a curve or open hair lines, and there is considerable room for personal elaboration on the finish of the ascenders and descenders. The thickening at the ends of the thin arms of the a, c, k, r and s can be rolled to the roundness of the dot of the i, and other letters can be persuaded to include a curled blob that pushes the whole texture of the text towards jolly dottiness. As with the other letter-styles it is the personal ones, developed over a lifetime of practice, that are often most interesting, especially those that are obviously done at speed without sacrificing quality. Some of these have progressed so far that they have returned halfway to their handwritten

manuscript origins – a success story for man over printed matter – but this is unusual, and most signwriters stick clearly within the rules made by the typefounders.

The term 'script', however, is generally applied to any lettering that is reminiscent of handwriting rather than mechanical printing, and it has a more inclined, flowing and running pattern than staccato typesetting. It clearly states that a human hand wrote it, although the effect can range from the formality of a royal command to the friendly and honest business signature of the chimney sweep. It always, however, flows along with a curving rhythm from left to right, and apart from any quality put over by the style of script used, it is this flow which is so useful to the signwriter in his range of ingredients.

The origins of today's signwriting scripts are, of course, in handwriting, but with two historic influences. The first is typography with its italic lettering, the sloping style produced by early printers to imitate the calligraphy of the papal scribes. This style became popular and was useful, but it developed quite formally amongst printers until it now seems more akin to static roman lettering than to handwriting, although the slope and more compressed pattern still remain.

(Above) This lower-case lettering in Knutsford church may be the same vintage as the Royal Arms shown in the photo on page 28, but the contrast is greater and the message is much louder, and prouder. Note the dished sides to nearly every main stroke, the sharp cut serifs and the pleasant spottiness caused by the curled blobs terminating so many of the letters.

(Left) This little caption plate is attached to a wooden barrel construction on display in the National Maritime Museum, Greenwich, and looks as if it were done very soon after the expedition – perhaps in relief at having returned at all. Not graceful, but personal, and fun.

The other, less constrained development took place in the parallel trade of engraving, where the accurate reproduction of artistic writing and drawing was improving dramatically. At the same moment that literacy was becoming more desirable and useful, and the art of writing more appreciated, the engravers were suddenly able to print fine examples of the writing-masters' work. From engraved copper plates they printed beautiful examples for the student to copy, and copy-book 'copperplate' writing was born. The engravers, however, were not content simply to emulate pen lettering, and pushed their new techniques to the extreme. Their tools do not have the directional constraints of a pen and can achieve extraordinarily fine, variable and graceful lines in any direction, and the occasional flourish of the seventeenth-century writing-master became a positive riot of rococo curls and scrolls in the work of the eighteenth-century engraver. The angle of the lettering leant much further to the right; when this style of calligraphy again became fashionable, it was only possible by the invention of a pen that held the nib at a more extreme angle to the paper. The high-spot of the ornate engraved work was during the eighteenth and

Signwriter's script on an old shop awaiting demolition in Gateshead in 1985, a double tragedy in this case because the neat signwriter's work is painted over a glass fascia panel, and the Victorian gold leaf sign could just be seen glinting through the peeling paint.

---

early nineteenth centuries, and much of the engraver's finest work was in the form of trade handbills and business cards for precisely the class of tradesmen for whom the emerging signwriter and sign painter was catering, as literacy and urban trade increased. It is not surprising that this copperplate style remains an important part of the signwriter's stock in trade, although its survival reflects much more recent change as well.

That same copy-book style, or a close descendant of it, was the standard handwriting encouraged in schools until the end of the use of dip-in steel pens, now entirely superseded by fountain, ball point and felt tip pens. All these can write with a uniform line in any direction, and this is a major change. Two physical properties of the old-fashioned pen nib helped to control the nature of copperplate writing, its sharpness and its springiness. It is difficult to make an upward stroke on paper

THE

Writing Masters

INVITATION, AND INSTRUCTION.

Come Youth, this Charming Sight behold,	Come Listen Youths, and I'll Display
With Lawrel Plum'd, a Pen of Gold;	To this Rare Art a Certain Way;
If You would win this Glorious Prize,	He that in Writing would Improve,
Do as Your Master shall Advise;	Must first with Writing fall in Love;
Till You, from Learners, Masters grown,	For True Love for True Pains will call,
Make both the Bays & Gold your Own.	And that's the Charm that Conquers All.

Three things bear mighty Sway with Men,	Who can the least of these Command,
The Sword, the Scepter, and the P E N;	In the First Rank of Fame will Stand

Labor Omnia Vincit

J. Champion   delin. et sculp.

Nᵒ IX.   G.B. sculp.

with a steel nib (or with a quill) without digging in and splattering ink everywhere, so all strokes must be made down or across the paper. By varying the pressure and pushing the points of the nib further apart, it is possible to create both thick and thin strokes and all variations in between. The direction and variation in pressure were the controlling factors that created such beautiful handwriting (and sometimes such appallingly messy handwriting) in the past, a technique and skill now rarely used and almost forgotten.

These skills were not forgotten, however, in the conservative world of traditional signwriters, many of whom were taught them at school. Some of their older customers haven't forgotten either and quite unconsciously ask for 'a bit of joined-up writing', recalling their first awareness of beautiful handwriting. Its popularity depends as much on the tradesman as the customer, however, and it is because it is satisfying to do that it survives. Copperplate is flexible, and can be done extremely fast by a practised hand, and so long as it looks right, rules can be bent and flourishes added to suit any space and taste. It contrasts well in texture and rhythm, and is quite evidently the result of hand-craftsmanship rather than machine, as a typefounder's letters have to be able to be added on to each other as independent units, whereas a calligrapher or signwriter can condense and overlap letters and words to suit the specific job. The signwriter's tools are well suited to the intention, and a pointed brush can emulate the pen line with great beauty; a powerful mixture of historic influence and practicality ensures graceful copperplate an important place in the art of signwriting.

The chisel-edged brush or the square cut

The Inns of Court in London have a continuing tradition of using this style of signwritten lettering, and every park gate and lawyer's entrance hall has examples of the handwriting fluency that constant practice brings to brush painted italic. Why ever did the honourable society not have their Highways Act notice signwritten as well, for neither sign helps the other?

'one-stroke' are very useful for painting versions of any pen letter, simply by keeping the angle constant and writing as if with a pen; but by twisting the brush as it moves it can also be made to paint an equal width stroke in any direction. An italic, or sloping, version of a simple sans-serif letter painted like this, with speed and urgency apparent in every stroke, is probably now the commonest letter in everyday use, and also probably reflects our business attitudes most accurately. This may be fine for a holiday advertisement, but is not so suitable on an insurance company board. From back-street garage to sea-front souvenirs, this 'Flash' lettering is insistently telling us to hurry before it's too late. . . .

At quite a different pace, old-fashioned

A page from one of the most popular copy books of the eighteenth century, *The Universal Penman*, with examples collected and engraved by George Bickham. The elaborate flourishes had a marked effect on gravestone decoration and the sloping handwriting became the standard pattern for two hundred years of school work.

The Art & Craft of Signwriting by William Sutherland

Gothic Blackletter, the Old English of the antique shop, still stands for history. In signwriting terms it has much both for and against it. On the positive side it is both quick and attractive; a practised writer with a one-stroke brush can letter with almost handwriting speed and with very decorative results – a strong vertical rhythm of thick strokes, with the weight of the short diagonal strokes at top and bottom giving linking horizontal zig-zag lines in opposition. With all the sharp hair lines crossing on the other diagonal, and the frills of the capitals, it is fun to do. The problem is that it can soon become almost illegible. It also has such a strong visual association with mediaevalism that it only comfortably fits a job when some quality of age is required – for example by 'Ye Olde Tea Shoppe' or the Cathedral Bookshop – despite the fact that the ancient classic roman can be used to reflect modern elegance quite successfully.

The purpose of this chapter has been to isolate and illustrate the basic forms of letter-

An old book title by a modern tradesman, an example of signwriters' copperplate by Ray Manning of Preston.

(Facing above) This horse-drawn pantechnicon uses a surprising number of different letter styles with varying degrees of success. The exaggerated blocking of 'Samuel Berry' on the side works handsomely, but the script-written 'Furniture Removers' below it looks very skinny and stretched, compared to its successful use on the back doors.

(Facing below) One word that says everything it needs to say, enhanced by the dropped shadow block lettering on the office window at Arpley station, Warrington.

(Above) Fast one-stroke lettering in Hull: cheap, but quite in keeping for some jobs.

(Facing above) An old-fashioned letter form on a new lorry from Edinburgh. Many road haulage firms from Scotland maintain very high standards of coachpainting, and still favour a very traditional treatment of lettering, panelling and lining that harks back to horse-drawn days.

(Facing below) Elegant shaded roman lettering and fine lining from the coach painting firm of Jennings and Co of Sandbach, Cheshire, who specialised in lorry-painting.

(Below) Perfect for pattern-making and pious thoughts in church, but a bit difficult to read. Variously known as Gothic, Blackletter or Old English, they are all based on medieval pen-lettering.

ing that the traditional signwriter commonly uses, but there are an infinite number of variations. Every signwriter develops a personal style eventually, one that will be recognised as clearly as a signature to others in the trade, and there are usually one or two particular alphabets which develop as the trademark. These individual, and sometimes extremely odd local lettering styles add particular character to an area, and can give great pleasure to those who have the eyes and interest to see them. Two examples, both in Cumbria, will illustrate this point, but it is true of many other small towns throughout the country.

In Cockermouth in 1983 one insistent style of lettering was apparent all over the place – on shopfronts, church notice boards and the ice-cream van. It was not the only style, but it was noticeable as being slightly odd, and quite particular, compared with the usual commercial or bad amateur signwriting also displayed around the town. Enquiries led to John Bell, recently retired, the town signwriter and ticket writer for more than thirty years. He is a man of wide experience, and quite capable of producing any sort of lettering demanded of him, ancient or modern; but the local businessmen, as is so often the case, assumed that he was the best qualified to design as well as paint their signs, and left him to solve the problems involved. His usual answer involves the use of wide, swelled-end sans-serif capitals, with some personal additions like the strongly curved underside of the mid-strokes of E and F, the slanting ends to the cross-stroke of the T, and a certain set of letter proportions that are as recognisable as hand-writing. Lower-case writing is often in a heavy pen-style script, reminiscent of Blackletter, written quite directly with one-stroke brushes. Although these usual letter-styles of his sometimes become clumsy or inappropriate, at other times the message, the style, and the space come together to make a sign of strong, satisfying simplicity.

In Ulverston, another group of letter-styles was to be seen throughout the town and the neighbouring area, all obviously painted by the same hand. Of the two commonest, the first was a very bold roman-based capital with hair line thin strokes and solid triangular serifs, the thick strokes sometimes lightened and decorated with a thin coloured line within them, and the whole face often blocked out.

One of Mr John Bell's immediately recognisable letter styles on a simple side street noticeboard in Cumbria. The wide proportions, and the fat curved tail to the C make this signwriter's own sans-serif as secure and comfortable as an armchair.

The second style, often used in conjunction with the first, was a very fancy 'fish-tail' Tuscan, swelling out to extra decorative bulges at the centres of the letter and creating a very rich pattern of writing, although still surprisingly easy to read. The craftsman was found to be Billy Gilpin, who had also recently retired. He was apprenticed in 1927 to one of the town's two main firms of decorators, but the death of the master signwriter long before Mr Gilpin was out of his time meant that he took over the signwriting work very young, and without much academic lettering tuition. With plenty of work and little competition, his own slightly unorthodox lettering developed over the years virtually unchallenged, either by more classical styles, or by price-cutting which would probably have forced him to reduce the amount of extra decoration and two colour blocking that he regularly used.

In both cases the tradesman's personal style has become the accepted local norm, and

each has become responsible for a large proportion of the lettering most often seen by the population of those towns. Their designs and craftsmanship have set local standards of unsophisticated public art, as well as reflecting the local attitude to business and people – their art is certainly popular and Mr Gilpin's work could happily be put in the class of folk art.

As may be guessed from the telephone number this is a very old window blind. Billy Gilpin, who painted it when he was a very young man, continued signwriting in Ulverston, Cumbria, throughout his working life and his personal lettering style is still to be seen throughout the town. The odd decorative bumps midway up the words 'Wholesale and Retail' grew through the years to become a very fat idiosyncratic Tuscan letter face that is entirely his own.

(Left) Mr Gilpin's own brand of Tuscan, near Ulverston, 1984.

4

TRICKS & TREATMENTS

CLOTHING THE BARE BONES

THE last section discussed the letter-forms in isolation, but although they should be regarded as the most important single ingredient, there are a whole range of design elements and tricks that make up the signwriter's palette. Just as a simple sign can be improved by a careful choice of letter, simple lettering can be used and enriched into a very complex and satisfying pattern by a sensitive craftsman. Conversely the very best lettering is spoilt by bad layout or thoughtless elaboration; taste and judgement still have to be exercised, whether it is a work of cheery popular art or a dour classical memorial.

A favourite trick of the signwriter, and a most traditional trick after 150 years at least, is blocking out, shading or 'raising' the letters. These are a range of related techniques but they all start from the illusion that the lettering is three-dimensional, sticking out or standing away from the background in some way so that it casts a shadow, or so that the imagined thickness can be seen. In itself the idea is rather silly, a clever deception that may cause some passing amusement when first encountered, but is soon ignored as it becomes more familiar. The sign-maker has never stopped using the technique, however, for it is a valuable way of enriching lettering and adding colour and texture to a simple sign. The original deception has become a straightforward decorative technique, and the only people

really deceived are the authors of signwriting books who – depending on the date of the book – give detailed construction and perspective diagrams or rant against the falsehood of the idea.

On the evidence of Nathaniel Whittock's book the idea seems to have started in the 1820s. He says that signpainters had recently begun to imitate 'the projecting letters of wood

---

A blocking and shading diagram typical of many from older signwriting and painting books, which make the common error of casting a shadow from the base of the letter on one side but from the face of the letter at the opposite side.

PERSPECTIVE

or metal that have of late become so fashionable'. More interestingly, he also mentions that painted lettering 'in bold relief' looks better than the real thing, but neither he nor later authors really discuss the reasons why it is more visually successful than one would expect from a mere imitation of letters made in a different way. By the 1880s Callingham speaks of blocked-out letters as those 'in which the modern signwriter delights', and devotes a careful section to the techniques involved. Twentieth-century authors progressively play it down as old-fashioned, try and discourage it as expensive and over-elaborate, but the public and signwriter both like it, and it persists stubbornly.

The first great friend of painted blocked-out lettering is the dull English weather, for a painted shadow accentuates the face of the letter regardless of the rain and whether or not it faces the sun. It also has the advantage of not having little corners for the water to collect in, which is where the rot starts.

The second ally would appear at first glance to be the signwriter's enemy, perspective. In reality it is not. In reality, a spectator standing directly in front of a line of relief lettering can see the thickness on the right-hand side of the letters at the beginning of the line, and on the left at the end. In the middle there is no actual thickness visible unless the spectator is looking up or down at it, or the lettering is casting a shadow from which the thickness can be deduced. This is fine in practice, because the spectator's eye is very experienced at understanding three dimensions and reads the

ELLIS'S

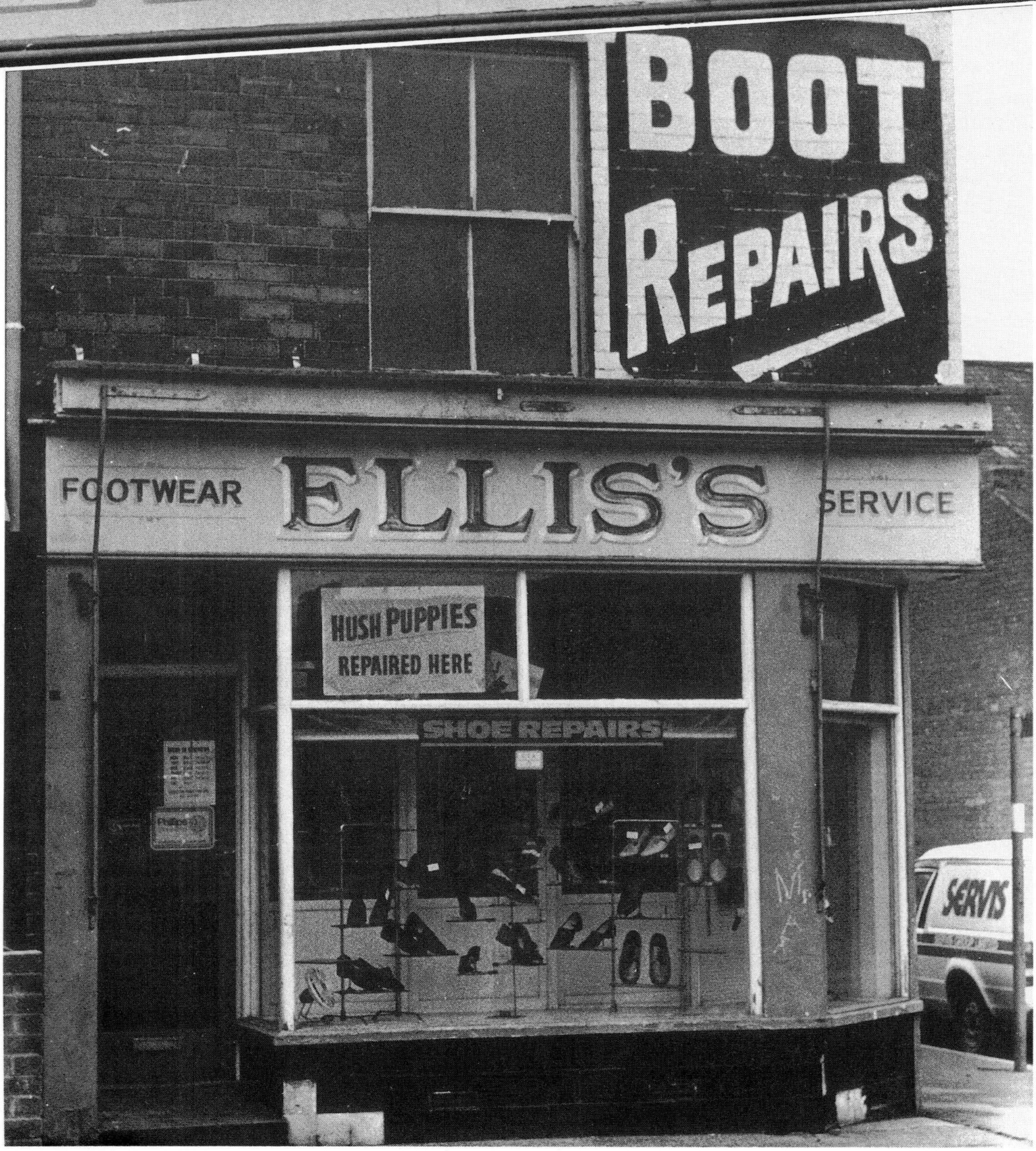
BOOT
REPAIRS
FOOTWEAR
ELLIS'S
SERVICE
HUSH PUPPIES
REPAIRED HERE
SHOE REPAIRS
SERVIS

lettering in sculptural terms, accepting and enjoying the changing relationship of the front of the letter to the background as the observer moves his viewpoint.

A painted version of the same wording presents a quite different problem. If it is painted strictly following the rules of perspective it can look totally convincing from one viewpoint, but conversely it must look wrong from every other; the lie becomes obvious because the apparent vanishing point does not move with the spectator, and one does not see more of one side and less of the other as one moves past it. This is only a niggling little problem, however, compared with that of the composition and spacing of the painted version. If it is viewed from the middle again, the first and last letters, with the thickness clearly visible down one side, will appear much more bulky as outline shapes than the same letters in the centre of the work, so spacing and balance are immediate problems. If the edge of the lettering is a different colour from the face, the difficulty is even more obvious, because each end of the word appears boldly in two colours whilst the middle is thin, and in a single colour. It can be fun as *trompe-l'oeil*, but it is uncomfortable as architecture for everyday business, or as a decorative pattern.

Signwriting makes a visual compromise, and gives each letter the same perspective, so that the same amount of thickness and shadow appears on each, and the layout can be balanced more easily. The odd thing is that having made this first concession to the reality of the painted surface, the signwriting authors

---

The main fascia lettering of this shop in Belvoir Street, Hull, uses nearly every painted addition possible – it is blocked out in two colours with a cast shadow on the background, and has the face of the letter recessed by an extra shadow line at the top and on the right. The central layout is standard, but stately, although rather overshadowed by the wall sign above which, because of its simplicity, has been painted up several times since it first appeared in 1935. The fascia was done in the 1950s. It was faded, but still clearly legible thirty years later.

continue their self-delusion that the painted letters trick the public. Callingham warns us that 'it is not for a moment to be supposed that thicknesses are to be introduced solely for the purpose of adding colour and giving variety to the work'. In fact, that is precisely what most signwriters do use it for. The concept of raised lettering gives the painter a respectable excuse to make a two-dimensional equivalent to the texture and effects of three-dimensional lettering, not necessarily an imitation of it. It is quite possible to deceive the eye, and is certainly done quite often, but blocking out is usually used as an honest ingredient in the making of flat signs, to produce fatter and more elaborate two-dimensional letters rather than as a pretence of three dimensions.

If a projecting letter is viewed directly from the front it is impossible to see the thickness, but it will still cast a shadow in a raking light. This is the reasoning behind the simplest and commonest form of shading, one colour painted down one side and along the bottom of each letter stroke, with the ends of each brush stroke cutting upwards at about forty-five degrees. It can be marked out by exactly drawing each letter shape slightly down and to one side of the original, with the two letters joined up diagonally, but in practice it tends to be done entirely freehand, and fast. Logically, according to the laws of optics and physics, a darker tone of the background colour should be used, but a firm contrast is often chosen to suit the overall colour scheme of the job.

This shadow, according to the same logic of reality, should be painted right up to the edge of the letter, but it rarely is. A gap is left between shading colour and letter, that effectively gives an outline of the background colour to two sides of the letter. This double change, background to shading to background to letter colour, adds a vibrancy almost like a halo that makes it stand out more clearly than the direct change from face colour to shading would, even though that contrast might be stronger. This distancing is most noticeable on the cheapest and fastest lettering jobs because, apart from the success of the effect, it is quicker and easier to do that way. Painting right up to the face needs more care than painting a roughly similar shape a few millimetres away from it, where a little irregularity is far less noticeable than if it broke up the clean edge of the letter shape. It is surprising, and rather unfortunate in some ways, how much a slick operator can get away with. Provided that the letters are neat and well-spaced, the additional elaboration of shading and blocking can be thrown on very roughly in approximately the right place, and will be accepted quite readily by the uncritical eye. That eye tends to see what the mind wants it to see, and if it is not insulted by lettering blatantly breaking conventions, it will accept sketchy shading as happily as a perfectly accurate representation.

If that same shading is carried out in two tones or two colours, a lighter one down the side and a dark below, it immediately achieves the simplest form of blocking out or 'raising', creating a painted view of the thickness itself. It is conventionally painted this way with the

---

The insistent repetition of the basic letter shape is more obvious when all the blocking and shading is reduced to a line design. The constant underlining and outlining round the letters becomes a complex pattern, but related firmly to the word.

bottom thickness visible as if looking up at it, but it can be viewed from left or right according to taste. There are minor advantages to both. If seen from the right, with the blocking or shading seen on the right of the letter, the thinner diagonal strokes of A, K, V and W of a strongly contrasted letter style are all strengthened by having the maximum amount of secondary colour running alongside them. If it appears on the left all the angles of the blocking are pushing up to the right, helping the lettering along with a suggestion of handwriting hurry, a hint of italic speed. Regardless of all this subtlety, it usually comes down to which side the signwriter finds it easier to do it on.

There was practically no limit to the complication and care that old-time craftsmen invested in raised letters in the past. The edges were painted with three or four beautiful tones of slow-drying colour, so that they could be blended together on the curves and in the corners, and every excuse for a shine or a shadow was stroked into the wet paint. Observed principles of landscape painting were absorbed into the imagined couple of inches of letter thickness; for example, colours and contrasts were sharper at the front of the letter than in the misty distance where it met the background. Highlights gleamed from every corner, and the triangular pattern of shadows

in the corners was repeated illogically on the blocking in full lighting. The shadow cast on the background by the thickness struck across in the other direction and provided extra contrast on the other side of the letter; it might be painted in two or three separate tones, the darkest in the corner near the letter, paler as it spread into the space between the letters. Whether or not they were aiming for super-realism, this technique of elaborating one essentially simple form by echoing it again and again in shadow and shape always achieved an extraordinarily complex pattern, like a geometric doodle, when all these tone and colour changes were translated into lines. In full colour it could be wonderful, glowing with light and colour, an icon to the competitive Victorian craftsman.

The commonest repeat of a letter shape is an added outline, and a simple border of contrasting colour is an attractive addition to any letter-form. The quality added depends on thickness and colour and can be anything from dignity to iridescence. It can be thick and obvious, itself a statement of style, or very thin,

Some distinguished outlined roman-based lettering in Hull, admirably suited to the architecture and the panel, with a thin black outline just sharpening the contrast with a dull green background. Note the subtle scroll-work too, a masterly understatement.

just a clarification of the letter shape. It can be a dark tone round bright lettering to sober it up, or a light edging to make it sparkle. A yellow border round red lettering on a white background is almost incandescent, but a black outline makes it very severe. Gold leaf lettering is usually outlined, particularly on light to mid-toned backgrounds because the gilt polish of gold varies quite dramatically from different angles in different lights, so a black outline is added to make the lettering clearly legible regardless of angle. It also has the bonus of tidying up the edge, which is difficult to produce perfectly with gold leaf alone, and makes it look very refined.

Like shading, outlining can be done very carefully and accurately right up against the letter colour, or kept an equal distance away to create a second 'negative' outline of the back-

A black outline going round a red letter on a cream door panel adds a touch of fairground for this modern theatre company van. Ray Manning at work in 1988.

ground colour. It can be done neatly and slowly (and expensively) or whipped round sketchily for a quick flash of seaside excitement. If the letter is a slim sans-serif and a thick outline is painted a full letter's thickness away, the result is a different letter made up of five stripes instead of an 'outlined' centre shape. Finally, of course, the middle can be left out altogether and the lettering painted in outline only, an attractive treatment which is coming into fashion again.

One of the pleasures of an outlined letter is that it is possible to use two letter-forms with different characters in one and the same place. The shape made by the outside of the outline will have different proportions from the inside shape; an equal thickness added all round a thin letter will result in a much chunkier style than that of the bone in the middle. The change is particularly pronounced with a classical seriffed letter at the

centre, as the delicate sharpness of the pointed serif becomes a more robust square-cut shape. The two styles of lettering thus formed are clearly related to each other, but have a distinct contrast of mood, a combination of elegance and strength within the same letter – a rare case of the signwriter being able to have his cake and eat it.

Scrollwork appears everywhere in English decorative art, and it has become a useful part of the signwriters' repertoire. It may be purely decorative, but scrollwork often plays an important part in filling a space and completing the composition of a sign. Just as a signwriter usually chooses and develops one or two letter styles that suit his nature, so he generally develops a personal pattern of scroll that will distinguish his work almost as clearly as a signature. There will be a limited group of brush strokes, a certain relationship of curves with which he feels happy, and that pattern will be adapted to suit any shape or space. It will have to vary to suit the style of lettering which it accompanies, and in some good examples seems to be a logical extension of the letter style chosen. The very best scrolls are probably those that are least noticed precisely because they appear as a natural extension to the writing.

A scroll or flourish is usually a finishing touch to balance the layout, or to relax the formality of austere lettering a little with a touch of beautiful nonsense. In certain cases, however, the scrollwork is allowed to take over as a more accurate representation of the mood or message than the actual words it accompanies, as on an ice-cream kiosk or fairground ride. Here the extrovert scrollwork expresses the good-time hopes of the proprietor better than words can do, a brassy over-decorated scroll conveying a cheery message complementary to the lettering. It is more difficult to appreciate the skill with which a more

subtle flourish enhances a less strident message until you see a crude or badly designed scroll clashing with the written message. Many otherwise appropriate signs are ruined by the addition of superfluous or ill-conceived scrolls.

The basic shape with which we are dealing, the natural unwinding curves of a double-rolled strip of paper, does not occur in nature very often, although hints of this decorative device are abundant. It is largely a human in-

---

The top word is the classical ancestor disguised with a bold outline to become a footed roman, whilst the lower one is a more ghostly outline. Between them is a skinny sans-serif letter outlined with a letter thickness, a thickness away, to give a very jolly set of stripes.

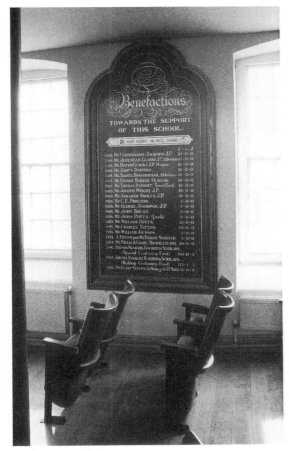

The calligraphic origin of the scrollwork is very clear on this board in the large Sunday School building in Macclesfield, Cheshire. The last date shown is 1942 but this may have been added to an older sign. It has a very satisfactory shape and layout.

leaves and tendrils. It can be adapted to fill the smallest space or expanded into a continuous border of any length, like the wave pattern that was known to the ancients as the 'running dog' scroll. In the best signwritten work there is a tense balance between the springing energy of the spiral and the relaxed curves of foliage, a beautiful equilibrium between graphic elements, all bound up in the curves of a practised brush stroke. In the worst work there is a wriggly lumpiness.

There have been three main influences on the development of the signwriters' scroll; the classical, the heraldic and the calligraphic. Its classical ancestry can be traced back to Ancient Greece, where the volute was a significant element in temple architecture. The difference between a volute and a simple spiral seems slight when described in words, but it is as different in quality as good wine is to flat beer. A spiral is a curve which continuously recedes from its centre by the same amount each revolution, resulting in a line running exactly equidistant from itself, whereas the curve of a volute moves from its centre by a constantly increasing amount. Whilst the first gives a mechanical design, the second produces a line of natural growth and tense power. Volutes combined with stylised foliage were used in the ancient classical architecture, which has exerted such an enormous influence on our everyday lives ever since the Renaissance.

The new classically based architecture of Europe after 1500, particularly popular in Britain in the eighteenth and nineteenth centuries, demanded new furniture and decoration in a similar style, and the ancient ruins and monuments were studied anew. Apart from naturalistic statuary, the decoration most popularly developed was the scrolled foliage of the Corinthian order of architecture, a plant that has been identified as Acanthus, a variety of thistle found in Greece. It is so stylised that the botany matters very little; it was the pattern made by the leaves and their serrations that were important to the decorator, with the extra

vention, a symbol of a natural idea discovered and used in prehistoric times, and one which has flowed from the pen, brush, or hammer and chisel at some time in every craftsman's work ever since. It can be interpreted as a symbol of growth and rebirth, of continuous but ever-changing natural processes, as it disappears within itself or flowers out from tight curved confinement; it contains elements of the shell structures of snail, winkle and whelk, combined with the unfolding vitality of young

(Above) A scroll design dashed on the frontboard of a farm wagon at the Reading Museum of Rural Life – a lovely swirl of confident decoration by Mr Biles from Bridport, from about 1945.

stress that the ribs of the leaf give to the growth curves. When it was imported to Britain as part of the Italian package it soon intermeshed with the Gothic love of rich textures and curling ivy patterns to produce a smothering excess of curls and rococo curves. New brooms kept trying to sweep back to classical simplicity, but the virulent acanthus scroll kept a firm popular root, and smothered everything in the nineteenth century from woven cloth to cast iron lamposts. Rich acanthus scrollwork was synonymous with well-educated success, and echoed the escapist dream of the working class on fairground rides and pub windows.

Further encouragement for this all-pervading fashion came from heraldry, the folk art of the aristocracy. A fully armoured medieval knight wore a cloth over his helmet and shoulders as a protection from the heat, held in position by a circlet of twisted fabric jammed over the helmet. The garment – the *lambrequin* or

A pair of volutes above a pair of spirals, with an edging of the ancient 'running dog' scroll.

This diagram of the capital and base of a Corinthian pillar from Rome is from an 1897 book on the *Orders of Architecture* by R. Phene Spiers. This classical blend of Ionic volutes with acanthus foliage is the basis of much scrolled decoration in signwriting as well as architecture and other applied arts.

---

mantling – is supposed to have been slashed in battle, in the romantic mind at least, and the gallant remains are represented in the formal art of heraldry as a mass of swirling drapery. In a correct achievement of arms, the mantling only needs to be a symbol, but heraldic artists ever since the sixteenth century have seized the excuse of elaborately bordered or slashed mantling to frame or unify the heraldic design with two colour scrollwork remarkably similar to the acanthus foliage of architecture. In the art of the heraldic engraver they are virtually indistinguishable. It may seem a peripheral influence in the twentieth century, but at the beginning of the nineteenth the work of the heraldic artist was everywhere, on the gates of big houses and the signs of small pubs, painted on windows and on elaborate funeral hatchments in every church, and it is not so surprising that it became a common decorative device across all class boundaries. When the official rules of heraldry were bent to the service of trade union and church banners in the late nineteenth century, acanthus scrollwork and heraldic mantling became interchangeable, and remained so until the end of traditional banner painting in the 1960s.

The third influence at work on the signwritten scroll, the calligraphic one, is again from the engraver, with his version of the squiggles and swirls of the copperplate writingmasters transferred to trade cards and handbills. The capitals are already quite elegantly decorative, but their loops and flourishes were often extended out over the wording or into the spaces between words to turn the whole block of lettering into an interconnected linear design. Scrolls and loops then need to be invented to fill spaces into which the capitals cannot logically be extended, and they immediately become a new design ingredient instead of an extension of the letter-forms. This is just one step away from a decorative scroll appearing as an independent unit, to be used by the designer or signwriter as he thinks fit to complete the artistic composition of his sign. It seems a pity that scrollwork is not as fashionable as it was, for there were occasional moments when the space available, the style of the sign, the writer's skill and what he had for breakfast combined to magical effect, and a scroll flowed from the brush with an ease that equalled any Japanese Zen brush-stroke art.

The term 'scroll' has so far only described the separate curled line decorations used as space fillers, or as extensions to the alphabet in some cases, but the other meaning, as in a scroll of parchment, also has a place in signwriting design. With its close relation, the ribbon or riband, it provides a wonderful design excuse to introduce sweeping lines of colour and lettering in any direction and in any

space. Starting from the concept of a strip of cloth or paper rippling in the wind like a flag, the signwriter is able to bend his band of colour right across the signboard or fold it up into a corner. The coils of spare material beyond the lettering can be rolled, twisted or folded to fill any available space, and can add the same powerful spring tensions as a piece of independent scrollwork. The advantage is in the laying in of a great swathe of contrasting colour, itself a new background for a different style of lettering.

It is a rather dated technique, but powerful

This Sunday school banner from the turn of the century must surely be the most extreme use of scroll-work, ribbons, and rococo cartouche outside the fairground. Every word is milked for rhythm and pattern from the highlights and shadows of the blocking, and when painted and gilded onto silk an amazing theatrical statement is made out of what is, after all, only an address. (Photograph from the John Gorman collection.)

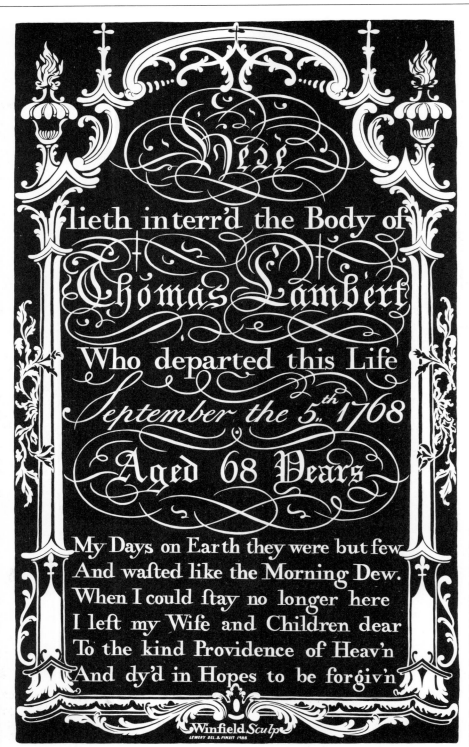

Here lieth interr'd the Body of Thomas Lambert Who departed this Life September the 5th 1768 Aged 68 Years

My Days on Earth they were but few
And wasted like the Morning Dew.
When I could stay no longer here
I left my Wife and Children dear
To the kind Providence of Heav'n
And dy'd in Hopes to be forgiv'n

Winfield Sculp.
LEWERY DEL. & PINXIT 1988

Calligraphic scrolls and flourishes transfer very well to letter cutting in a smooth stone, evident in this Leicestershire slate from Clifton graveyard near Nottingham. The stonecutters often sign their work, but some are not sure whether they are sculptors or engravers, and others just put *fecit*.

Fig 1. RIBBANDS FOR SIGNWRITERS.
Fig 2. Fig 3.
DECORATORS. ART R. JONES DEPT
Fig 4. 75
THE SHOP FOR QUALITY
6
5 Fig 5 & 6 Showing Reduction
Fig 7. Dowling.
Fig 8.
H. Voller. Decorator.
Fig 9.
GEO. ROUTLEDGE
PUBLISHERS & PRINTERS
Fig 10.
Fig 11 DECORATIVE 1916 HENRY ASHWIN Sign Writer

A page of ribbons from a decorators' book of 1916
by Henry Dowling, which offers many interesting
variations of layout for the sign artist to design with.

none the less, and recurs most often in traditional work on lorries and fishing boats. It is a useful device to frame a word or two inside an interesting silhouette of colour, a good panel for a house name or boat name on a large expanse of wall or a wheelhouse. The reverse side of the scroll, where it appears in the folds and counterfolds, may be painted in another contrasting colour to create an even more striking block of colour against the background. The ribbon is usually painted to represent a silky material, with plenty of sheen and shading on the curves, and can bring a

rich touch of pageantry to an everyday sign, like a silk Sunday-school banner in a cobbled street. These banners themselves, along with their trade union counterparts, made much use of painted ribbons to carry the wording, sweeping over the central pictures and entwining with the flanking acanthus scrollwork – interesting examples of visual design with spiritual function, of lettered messages with uplifting mood.

With all their convolutions, the design of such banners is invariably symmetrical, precisely balanced either side of the centre line, and most 'traditional' signwritten work follows this pattern. Fashions for gimmicky and off-centre layouts come and go but the accepted baseline for conservative customers is still centrally arranged wording in a rectangular panel. There is such comfort and security in this layout that it must have some deeper significance than simply unimaginative convention, and it has outlived all the sweeping layout changes of the 'gay nineties', 'Bauhaus thirties' and 'contemporary fifties'. Signs that appear ludicrously out of date now are precisely those that were right up to the minute then, turning their back on tradition in order to shout their presence at the time.

So many influences make us regard a straight line of lettering as the normal and expected one that any variation has a lot of power. We learn to read from books which are typeset in straight lines, and our square-cornered architecture encourages square-panel thinking, reinforcing our innate feeling that a combination of horizontal and vertical is strong and safe. Lettering that is straight and horizontal is so normal that it can hardly be said to make any sort of a visual statement, but variations undoubtedly do. Diagonal words have a certain dash and hurry to them, a bit daredevil if they rise up from the left, rather steadier and more believable if they drop to the right. Arched lettering has a little of both with an architectural feel, like the pediment of a temple, words asking to be seen as a grand statement, bridging a gap in our knowledge.

Double curves are on the point of being gaily out of control, and hint at temptation rather than information to modern eyes. The Victorians were more adventurous in their approach, and some of their involved layouts and contrasts of lettering now seem quaintly at variance with the purpose of the signboards' messages, even though as pieces of abstract artistic composition they could be amazing.

These two gilded glass door panels in Okehampton, Devon, seem totally at variance with the security of the door itself as the words wander about. It's probable that the larger glass panels below once bore lettering as well, which would probably have made a more stable design.

(Below) These signs were illustrated in a 1914 *Decorators and Painters* magazine, presumably as examples of current taste. The asymmetrical and curving layout of the left-hand one seems far too jolly for its subject, although they are interesting pieces of design in their own right. They were painted by Mr H. E. Spencer of Crown Street, Liverpool.

Lettering arranged vertically is difficult to read at speed, and it is not a good way to promote an unusual or important message. There are, however, a number of words that are easily recognised when read from top to bottom, words like CAFE, TAXI, or HAIR-DRESSER. This is partly because one 'reads' the familiar pattern of certain letters put together, and partly because they are so commonly used that way that it is almost traditional to those businesses. They often operate from small premises where sign space is limited, and because they do not have obvious materials for exciting window displays, those words have always formed an important part of the outside shop image, working as both information and decoration. The recent addition to the ranks of instantly recognised image-words is SEX SHOP, particularly since public sensibility has caused the contents to be decently hidden within a plain frontage.

Individual letters placed out of alignment within the line have a similarly disproportionate effect on the mood of the message. A jiggly arrangement of letters can vibrate with anything from emotional tension to uproarious abandon, charged with almost uncontrollable energy. It can work for horror or happiness, but as the signwriter rarely needs to evoke horror, its main use is for signs advertising holiday and party business, anything from hot dogs and holiday flatlets to the hall of mirrors at the fun-fair. Seaside resorts provide lots of examples reflecting and helping the holiday hopes of the tripper, a bit tipsy and uninhibited, but still clean and bright and clear enough to read.

The colours, too, can help. The seaside signwriter uses lots of white and pale blue backgrounds with pale blocking colours, as if to exaggerate the brightness of the sky and the need for sunglasses. Red and yellow are the favourite lettering colours, with some blue; but green is rare, as if it is felt to be out of place on a sun-baked promenade. A few five-pointed stars scattered in any available space can add the final sparkle to these seasonal boards.

One of the vertical words that the public will immediately recognise rather than read is 'Hairdressing'. This example near a busy roundabout in Worcester also illustrates the barber's lettering taking over and becoming a window display of stripes and stripy lettering, a modern version of the barber's pole tradition.

Staid permanence is not called for when you are enjoying a week's holiday, and this fresh 'up-to-the-minute' image means that many seaside letter styles owe much to the speedy but more temporary work of the ticket writer. Translucent bright colours on a white background, lots of outlining with unnecessary use of underlining, and inverted commas to make the effect more staccato, all add up to a latent excitement that will burst out at the drop of a lunchtime drink. Using every trick of design and layout with handwriting speed and confidence, the very best of this work is a visual expression of these holiday feelings, working on a different level from the direct meaning of the words, and a work of art in its own right.

5

STIMULATING SIMULATION

PURE GOLD TO MOCK MARBLE

ONE of the signwriter's most respected skills has always been his ability to use gold leaf, either as a surface treatment or on glass where its full mirrored glory is shown at its most spectacular. Gilding has a long history back to the ancient Egyptians, and until recently was regarded as a separate specialist job, but changing taste and increased cost has left the signwriter as one of the few remaining regular users of this lovely material. The world is so used to regarding gold as an abstract concept, a rate of exchange used instead of barter, that it is easy to forget (or never even consider) how it ever reached this fabulous value in the first place, rather than brass washers or cowrie shells. Rarity is part of the value of course, and the fact that it has to be dug out of solid rock with great labour, but this applies to many other materials too. What is so extraordinary, after its visual beauty, is its immutability, its resistance to change. It looks good and stays looking good for ever, and thus takes some of the mythological immortality of a god, worthy of worship itself. Gold is relatively soft, with a low melting point, and is easy to work, but it is also amazingly ductile and can be beaten into incredibly thin sheets without losing its beauty or permanence.

Incredibly thin indeed, for a sheet of gold leaf, made from one of the heaviest metals in the world, is so thin that it will blow away with a gentle breath. It will stick to the natural grease of the cleanest fingertips, without obscuring the tiniest detail of the fingerprint, and needs considerable practice to be handled successfully. It is made by goldbeaters who

These suggestions in Cassell's *House Decoration* of about 1900 mix classical acanthus with a design that would not look out of place in iron on a medieval church door.

Fig. 773.

Fig. 774.

Fig. 775.

Figs. 773 to 775. Scrolls for Sign Writers.

place small squares of thin gold about as thick as a cigarette paper between pieces of skin, traditionally made from the large intestine of an ox, and beat a pile of skins and gold with a hammer until the gold spreads out to four or five times its original area. Then it is cut into quarters and the process repeated, and repeated again. The resulting gold leaf is so thin that when it is attached to tissue paper and held up to the light it appears translucent, even though the material itself is extremely dense. Because the gold reflects all the red-orange-yellow colours of the spectrum, the translucency appears as a most beautiful blue, quite a shock to normal expectation. It has not, however, lost its permanence, and gold leaf correctly applied to lettering on a signboard will outlast all the background colours; and I have seen very old pub-signs that were nothing but a rusty iron sheet, except for the lettering which had been gilded and which still stood out from the surface where the gold had protected the underlying layers. The traditional street sign for a goldbeater's workshop is a gilded muscular arm holding up a hammer, for all the beating was done by hand, and each batch needed six or seven hours beating. Mechanisation has helped the process recently, but the final beating still has to be done by the hand craftsman, and the expense of gold leaf is due as much to labour as to the cost of the raw material. An ounce of gold will beat out to cover an area about twelve foot square, the size of a living-room carpet, which is an awful lot of lettering. Luckily it is still cheap enough, in tiny amounts, to remain in use for lettering.

There are substitutes, and there are cheaper ways of getting a similar result, but being cheaper they are not so good or so permanent. Gold powder can be mixed with a medium and used like a paint, but the surface is slightly granular and behind a film of varnish. Dutch metal looks like gold for a while, but as it is a mixture of zinc and copper it very soon tarnishes badly, as do bronze powders that can be dusted on to tacky varnish to achieve a gold

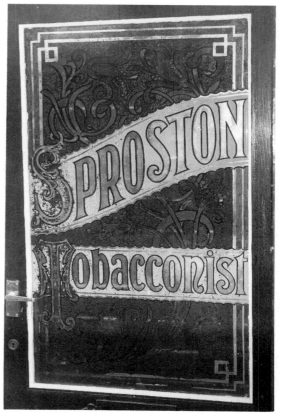

This shop door panel in Northwich, Cheshire, was painted in 1906 and survived in situ until the 1980s, but when the business moved it was removed and is now preserved inside their new premises. The brightly painted background design has darkened considerably with age but the gold-leaf work is still excellent.

---

effect. Both need protecting by varnish, but it follows that their life is only as good as the varnish that covers them, and the same applies to the various silver finishes, either actual silver leaf, or the more common aluminium leaf. They are, however, wonderfully reflective undercoatings for coloured glazes painted on top; fairground painters use a special range of flamboyant varnish colours over silver leaf for some stunning colours, as well as for a gold substitute.

The principle of gold leafing is simple – you

The fanlight window above the front door has always been a favourite place for the house name and number, and many have survived in Edwardian terraces. This grand example in Princes Avenue, Hull, doubles as a professional signboard as well.

---

stick it on with glue – but the practice is rather more subtle. The 'glue' for surface work is generally a varnish-based substance which is allowed to dry to a precise state of hardness and tackiness that just holds the gold to perfection – too dry and the leaf will not stick properly, too wet and the gold may wrinkle and crack. The gold is so thin that it reveals and exaggerates any flaws beneath it, and if it is done in a dirty place the final job will show up lots of bits of gold-plated dust and rubbish, for the gold is only as shiny as the size that holds it. Unfortunately the shiniest oil varnishes are the slowest drying, and are thus

most likely to collect dust from the atmosphere, so great care has to be taken over cleanliness for a really first-class job. The gold comes from the goldbeater in little books with a 3¼-inch square leaf of gold between each page. The leaves are slid from the book onto a powdered leather-covered pad, spread out and cut up with a blunt but immaculately clean knife, and the pieces transferred to the job with a wide but thin brush called a gilder's tip. This has the merest hint of grease at the tips of the hairs, picked up from rubbing it across the face or hair, which is sufficient to make the gold stick to it just long enough to carry it from the cushion to the prepared gold size on the signboard. The gold leaf almost leaps off the tip and onto anything stickier – not necessarily the intended destination. Just to complicate the job, the gilder dare not breathe heavily, however much his heart is beating, or the gold will be blown into the air irrecoverably. It is obvious even from this very sketchy description that gold leafing is a technique that needs much patience and a lot of practice, but the rewards are great. The techniques used have been comprehensively described in several of the older books for the signwriter listed in the bibliography, and very clearly and usefully in the one modern publication, Bill Stewart's *Signwork*, which is thoroughly recommended for practical advice. One demonstration is worth a thousand words, though, and the first few fumbling experiments with the real thing are far more use than photographs.

Gold leaf is also supplied pressed onto slightly waxed paper when it is known as 'transfer gold'. It is much more manageable this way as it can be used outside in a breeze, and also more economical, as each sheet can be pressed accurately on to the tacky surface. When the tissue paper is pulled away the gold stays only on the gold size, whilst the surrounding leaf stays on the transfer paper and can be used on the next letter. The liquid called gold size is generally preferred as glue on outside work, because it dries very fast,

Worthing signwriter Derek Pond using transfer gold leaf on a shop front in Brighton, Sussex, aptly titled 'Fine Artworker'. The lettering has been coated with gold size and allowed to become tacky and the gold leaf, loosely attached to tissue paper, is here being pressed on to it from the back of the paper.

before the dust and dirt can get to it; but it dries with a matt surface, so the gold is never quite so bright as on the slow-drying oil size.

For long life and the ultimate in brilliance, however, the signwriter brings two of mankind's most permanent materials together – gold leaf and glass. Because it is so thin the lustre of gold leaf is only as good as that of the surface to which it adheres, but when it is attached to the back of glass the visible surface seen through the glass is as polished as the surface of the glass, in exactly the way that the silvering of a mirror works. There is a glue film between the gold and the glass to hold it

on, but it is so fine as to be almost infinitesimally thin and invisible. The technique is to put a wash of very dilute gelatine over the clean glass and then to lay on loose gold leaf all over the area to be gilded, with a generous overlap at the edges. The gold spreads out flat over the wet size, which drains away and dries in a few minutes to allow the gold to take on the surface contours of the highly polished glass. This can be improved further by gentle burnishing, polishing and scalding until the face side, seen through the glass, is like a golden mirror. When that is thoroughly dry the actual design of lettering or pattern is painted in reverse on the back, directly over the gold in a tough resistant paint, and allowed to dry. Then the extra gold round the edges can be rubbed off with cotton wool and warm water, leaving on the glass just the lettering or design which has been painted in with the protective backing-up paint. The results of the simplest application of this technique are to be seen in every town, for it has become a tradition of the legal and medical professions to have their names and businesses in gold on their business windows. Doctors, dentists and solicitors throughout the country soberly proclaim themselves with restrained elegance in gold and black, and estate agents, too, hope that something of the same dignity will rub off on their more brazen image by using gold lettering on the shop window. The height of this gold-on-glass fashion was, not unexpectedly, the prosperous period that ended with the First World War, but what is more surprising is how short its history was prior to that. William Sutherland says in his introduction of 1860 'writing and ornamenting in gold and silver leaf on glass is . . . of recent date . . . and is only in its infancy as regards its application to the useful and ornamental Arts. I am myself applying it to purposes which were not thought of a few years ago; and I feel convinced that, when its importance as a medium of decoration is fully known, it will be most extensively applied.' He was right. Each later book on signwriting gave increasingly comprehensive

This design is acid-etched onto a pub window in Northwich, Cheshire, although the diagram does not do justice to the various grades and textures involved, nor to the thoughtful touch of colour painted on the lettering afterwards. Probably done soon after 1903 when the pub changed its name from *The Lion* to *The Lion and Railway*.

instructions and complex recipes, and the trade of glass-writer acquired a mystique of its own. Luckily for us, the materials and techniques were so good that some very fine examples have survived, a few in museums, but many still *in situ* on long-established chemists' and butchers' shops throughout the country. Clockmakers and jewellers naturally ally themselves with the rich glitter of gold, and they provide more modern examples in

(Facing above) A graceful advertisement for high-quality work in Reading done by Maurice Thake, whose father founded the firm here in 1905.

(Facing below) A small, friendly house name board from the Thake studio, just across the street from the workshop itself in Reading.

(p.98) A rich mixture of lettering and patriotic heraldry on an old showcloth now preserved in the Polka Children's Theatre collection in London, showing successfully all the tricks of the trade in excess.

(p.99 above) Baroque still rules this ride as the lettering on Armstrong's Waltzer bursts out into gold-leaf scroll-work and foliage at every opportunity.

(p.99 below) This lettering is certainly not graceful, but the higgledy-piggledy layout packs a powerful funfair punch. This was in 1974, and obviously succeeded, because Armstrongs now use the same layout in huge chrome-plated letters.

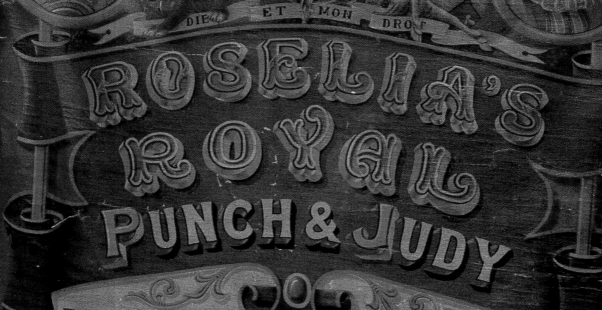

DIEU ET MON DROIT

ROSELIA'S
ROYAL
PUNCH & JUDY

PATRONIZED BY ALL NATIONS

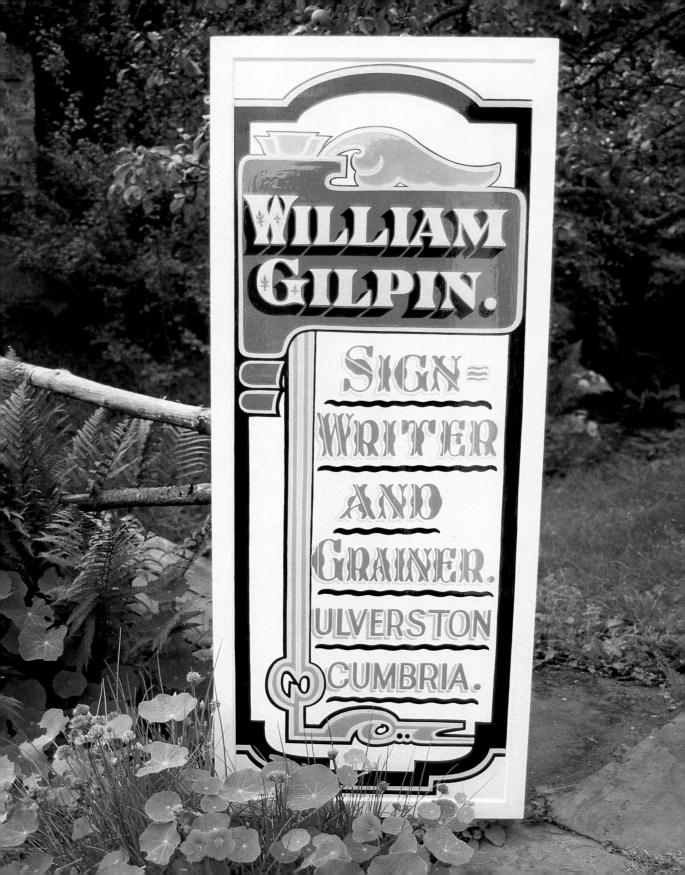

most towns, but it is a time-consuming and expensive technique and rather confined to the luxury end of the market. The coach trade likes to show off a bit, however, and there are good examples of glass gilding on the narrow name panels across the back of many holiday coaches, hurrying to Morecambe or the races.

Closely allied to glass-gilding is glass-embossing, making designs and lettering on windows by burning away the polished surface with hydrofluoric acid. This is another long process made doubly exciting by the fact that the acid burns clothes and skin as well as glass, and the fumes are dangerous to the eyes and lungs; it has dropped out of favour somewhat. The principle is to paint out all the areas of glass that need to remain clear and polished, and then to flood the remaining areas with the acid, which etches away the surface. By varying the time and adding various ingredients, a whole range of textures are possible, from a milky translucence to a heavy granular appearance. After cleaning the glass again these surfaces can in turn be gilded or painted and a tremendous range of effects achieved. Similar though more limited effects were obtainable by sand-blasting the surface through a stencil or a protective coating, and although it sounds like an industrial process, someone had to cut the stencil or paint on the protection. The best examples are often seen in pubs but there is often good and less ostentatious work to be seen in the front doors of old-fashioned outfitters. Both glass-gilding and embossing rely on the preparation of a design in advance, so there is little chance of any immediacy or spontaneity in the work, but for pure craftsmanship the best work of the golden age of the late nineteenth century will never be surpassed, for it is simply superb.

Another decorator's technique much favoured in the past was 'graining', the imitation of natural wood grain and markings with paint, and it used to be common for a man to

This acid etched design is on the window panel of a shop door in Todmorden, West Yorkshire. It is an odd photograph because it is a negative print from a slide, printed very dark to show up the lovely flowing design of handsome lettering and scrollwork.

advertise himself as 'Signwriter and Grainer to the Trade'. He offered his services in these two specialities to decorating firms which did not themselves have sufficient work to keep such a specialist fully enough employed to justify his higher wages. Such a man, however, might be kept busy between three or four companies, without the responsibility of an entirely independent business and with the added job satisfaction of varied challenging work.

A remarkably pleasing noticeboard illustrating Mr Gilpin's most usual letter-forms.

Gold lettering with a matt centre, with the black backing paint overlapping the edge of each letter to become an outline or shadow on part of an old shop front in Smithdown Road, Liverpool. Although badly cracked it was later successfully removed in one piece and restored.

Graining was popular throughout society, and the skill was widespread. At the top of the scale were men who specialised in graining alone, men whose skill was quite frighteningly perfect. The gold-medal winning Thomas Kershaw, whose 1851 exhibition panels are now displayed at the Victoria and Albert Museum in London, was such a man. At the other end was any ordinary painter who was expected to be able to brush-grain the seats in the tap-room adequately with a worn-out dusting brush. Between the two was the signwriter/grainer, well-practised with small brushes and colour, and with an observant and sometimes artistic eye. Although the detractors of graining always quote Ruskin's antipathy to pretence and disguise, and it can certainly be a perfect imitative sham, it is also a pattern-making technique that can be tasteful in tone, texture, pattern and colour, all manipulated by the grainer to suit his own sense of design. It is practical and long-lasting, for the transparent brown scumble rubbed into a matt lead undercoat, covered by varnish, actually protects woodwork very well. It disguises flaws and does not show markings or dirt easily, and the translucent colour improves with age and later varnishing. Grained doors, particularly house front doors, were the mainstay of the trade, and there are some areas of the country still fortunate enough to have a tradesman at work, with customers still demanding the time-honoured technique.

An unadorned roman letter with the most restrained engraver's flourish seems to suit this business. Gilding on glass by Mr Cave, about 1928, in Bromyard, Worcestershire.

Oak is the favourite, and is popular with the grainer for it offers the opportunity to make strong visual designs out of the 'figuring', the wriggly cross-markings of the medullary rays apparent in a real oak plank cut for high-class joinery work. For signboards the darker richer colours of walnut and rosewood make better backgrounds to lettering, but the wavy texture of the graining can be rather disturbing to the clarity of the writing if it is done crudely. Oddly, it is sometimes done as a backing-up treatment behind lettering on glass, a real *tour de force* for a show-off grainer working backwards.

Partnered with the art of graining is that of marbling, sometimes also seen as a glasswork back-up treatment, and with the closer affinity of glass to marble it is generally more successful. Painted marble has a long history, but its greatest days were probably in the eighteenth century, when the interiors of many large mansions, with plaster arches and wooden pillars, were painted to imitate classical Greek or Roman architecture. It was very generally popular throughout the nineteenth century, but it really only survived into the twentieth on fireplaces and shop fronts, decorating the panels of the pilasters on either side. Now, it only appears, tongue-in-cheek, on the plywood balustrades of the funfair.

A general signwriter might also have been expected to make the board itself, although a larger workshop would have employed a carpenter or joiner. What is particularly interesting in so much older work is the variation from the simple rectangular shape of most modern sign-written boards. There are the short-term fashions in board design, like fashions in lettering, but there is also a body of architectural boards, where the sign bears some relationship to the style of the building. Boards with arched tops, or built into window recesses, or curved on a corner, or standing high up breaking the skyline, were all designed for that one place, setting the signwriter a unique set of problems each time. The survivors now are unusual, but a close study of almost any photograph of a Victorian or Edwardian city street shows dozens of such varied sign shapes. Just as the more elaborate lettering was asking for extra attention in a crowded street, so any variation in shape that could set a sign one step above its neighbour gained customers for both the shop and the signwriter.

Photographs of old pubs show many of the best examples, and recently some major breweries have belatedly discovered that the quality and style of their signs form a major part of the outward appearance of their pubs. This obvious fact, so long in re-emerging, has given a much-needed boost to many old-fashioned signwriting skills. The first stage was the rediscovery and use of old-style typefaces in their advertising in the sixties, particularly Watney Mann's use of the Cooper Black typeface, which was so successful that it was soon copied in various ways all over the country. It has taken the designers another twenty years to discover that other, larger, aspects of signboard design and craftsmanship are also important in presenting an image of high quality and old-fashioned reliability. There is suddenly a noticeable increase in the amount of hand-painted lettering on pubs, and an encouraging rise in the overall quality of the signs used, both in shape and layout. The big breweries are now vying with each other to present the most traditional image using old-fashioned lettering and craftsmanship. Blocked and shaded lettering with gilded flowing script, complete with copperplate flourishes, are everywhere suggesting traditional beer, good food and romantic Dickensian hospitality. It is cheering to see signs designed and used as part of the architecture again, and to rediscover the fun of flamboyance after the severity of utilitarianism.

(Below) This glass fascia panel, from the High Street in Newport, Shropshire, shows gold autograph script backed up with some very rich graining. It is interesting because it is quite recent, for it is signed and dated by J. Stainer, June 1953.

(Facing above) A perfect blend of interesting signboard shape, to match the architecture, with a splendid layout and choice of lettering on the gate to complement both. Commercial Road, Whitechapel, in London.

(Facing below) This impressive modern gable-end sign in Lancaster is constructed of a number of separate units. The background shape with its arched centre is a panel plastered direct on to the wall whilst the lettering and pictures are on a series of smaller sections mounted just off the wall to create their own real, cast shadow.

ESTABLISHED 1814
Proprietor
R. M. SEYMOUR CHALK
J.J. & S.W. CHALK
TIMBER MERCHANTS & IMPORTERS
FINLAND WHARF, NEWELL ST. LIMEHOUSE. E14

J.J. & S.W. CHALK

J.J. & S.W. CHALK
ESTD 1814
TIMBER
MERCHANTS & IMPORTERS
AND BOAT
FINLAND WHARF, NEWELL ST. LIMEHOUSE. E14

MITCHELL'S
OF LANCASTER

The Greaves Inn

The Greaves Inn

TRY MITCHELL'S CONNOISSEUR BEERS
DARK MILD · SPECIAL BITTER · CENTENARY ALE

We have AMPLE CAR PARKING at REAR
REAL ALE & TRADITIONAL FOOD

BEERS BREWED the TRADITIONAL WAY WITH A GLINT OF OLD GOLD

6

ON THE STREET, ON WATER, AND IN THE FAIR

SIGNWRITING is done with paint and brushes, mainly on pieces of wood, and however good the craftsmanship, English weather fades the paint and rots the timber. Ordinary signwriting is ephemeral, and although a reasonable amount of old work survives, it is a very tiny proportion from which to draw historic conclusions. There are two linked temptations to be wary of: nostalgia, which suggests that because it is old it must be good, and the conclusion that because so much old work is of high quality, all contemporary work was equally good. This ignores the fact that part of the reason it survived is because it was

---

Lettering on the side of a winnower in the Hunday Farm Museum, Northumberland, presumably done about 1925 when the machine was new. Painted in black on grained woodwork, with some white shading whipped in.

well-made, well-designed and did its job. The rest has vanished because it wasn't and didn't.

As one would hope, the museums, as cultural guardians of the past do preserve historic examples of signwriting, but the best is often accidentally preserved by being on something like an old vehicle or shopfront, rather than preserved for itself alone. Where signs are displayed as exhibits they are on show as examples of high-quality craftsmanship and dated design, and the simpler unsophisticated stuff is left to be found by accident. Transport collections are good hunting grounds, and agricultural museums sometimes have fine lettering on their machines, but the best examples are probably in the various county folk museums. I only know of one museum with a signwriter's workshop exhibit, the Abbot Hall Museum of Lakeland Life in Kendal, which has an interesting display of tools,

A satisfying example of a late-Victorian or Edwardian shop that is sufficiently unmodernised to be still complete with the architectural details it was designed with. The neat unostentatious lettering of this one in Hull uses a standard central layout on the fascia that exactly suits the centre-doored architecture. White on bright red, but all a bit faded.

---

brushes, notebooks, pigment cabinet and paintmill, as well as local signs and signboards. In London, the Museum of London has plenty for those interested in lettering, as well as the old Guildhall Museum collection of pub signs, but the best discoveries are still to be made by serendipity, by walking the streets quite aimlessly but with lettering eyes wide open, looking on alley walls for 'no loitering' signs, on warehouse doors for loading-bay numbers and crane warnings. You may get some funny looks, though.

Shopfronts are still one of the richest sources of good-quality signwriting, though their numbers dwindle year by year. The architecture of the characteristic small English shop is basically classical in style, though heavily camouflaged with later fads and fashions. The medieval form was a hole in the wall with shutters, a window without glass, with a separate doorway alongside, but expansion of retail trading in the eighteenth century created a new fashion in shopfronts. It became another excuse for a temple from Ancient Rome, built with all the trappings of an architectural order, columns, entablature and pediment, although the pediment might be a three-storey house on top. The photograph shows how this unit evolved into an elaborate frame for a recessed central shop doorway flanked by display windows, the two outer columns becoming flat pilasters, and any central ones slimming down to window framing. The entablature supported by these pillars remains, the topmost mouldings of the

cornice cunningly concealing the roller blind whilst the frieze below it has expanded to carry the proprietor's name and trade, the part now generally termed the fascia board. This was once the key feature of the signwriter's shop work, a proud display of his skill and the shop-keeper's intentions, and the majority of towns have one or two shops surviving from the pre-plastic age, with a few more still continuing the signwriting traditions of their particular trade.

The standard layout is to have the shop owner's name in the middle in capital letters, flanked by words or phrases describing the business in smaller writing on either side. We are used to this arrangement and it seems almost natural to have writing over the door, but it is actually quite unnecessary. Customers choose their shops by window shopping more than by reading the fascia board, and most of

The classical ancestry of the humble shopfront is given away by the Composite style capitals above the flat pilasters supporting this fascia in Springbank, Hull. How nice for the signwriter that neither 'Watchmaker' or 'Jeweller' have any descenders to spoil that delicate underlining, making them perfect supporters for Mr Scott's name. A secure roman letter in two colours with a dropped shadow behind it completes this quiet masterpiece but, alas, the shop was closed and the 'for sale' notices were already up in 1987.

A signboard by Billy Gilpin of Ulverston, using his own decorative letter-forms to their best advantage to make an attractive but still readable mass of letters.

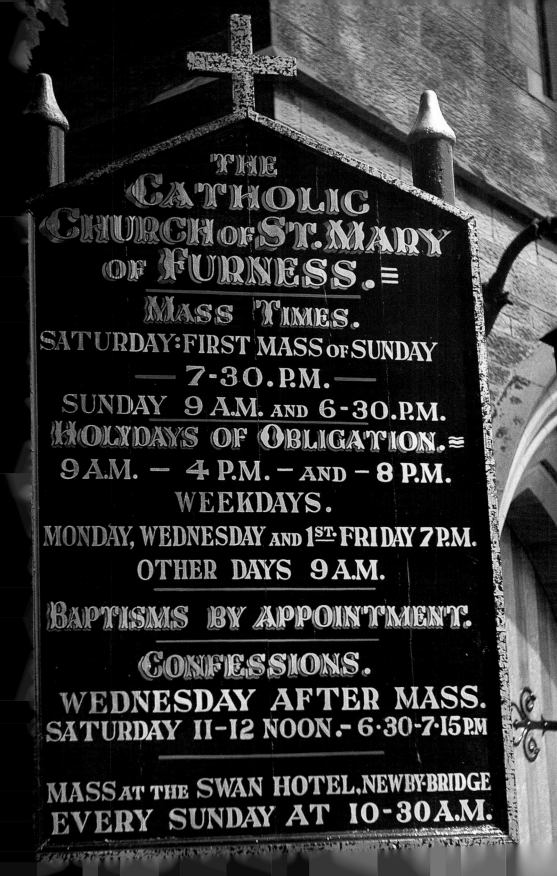

THE
CATHOLIC
CHURCH of ST. MARY
of FURNESS. =
MASS TIMES.
SATURDAY: FIRST MASS of SUNDAY
— 7·30. P.M. —
SUNDAY 9 A.M. AND 6·30. P.M.
HOLYDAYS OF OBLIGATION. ≈
9 A.M. — 4 P.M. — AND — 8 P.M.
WEEKDAYS.
MONDAY, WEDNESDAY AND 1ST. FRIDAY 7 P.M.
OTHER DAYS 9 A.M.

BAPTISMS BY APPOINTMENT.

CONFESSIONS.
WEDNESDAY AFTER MASS.
SATURDAY 11-12 NOON. — 6·30-7·15 P.M.

MASS at THE SWAN HOTEL, NEWBY·BRIDGE
EVERY SUNDAY AT 10·30 A.M.

them have been there dozens of times anyway. Certainly it is handy to be able to differentiate one shop from another, but the old signs and symbols could have done it. The Red Bull butcher's shop would be just as individual as the *Red Lion* pub, and a number on the door would be enough for the postman. The owners like to think that they were advertising their services but if they were really interested in catching passing trade they would do better to write up BREAD and CAKES in large letters instead of bracketing their own name with 'Baker and Confectioner' in delicate script. What is really being sold is an established personality, the promise of a personal relationship between proprietor and customer. The name is a sign of security for the careful shopper, an aspect sometimes reinforced by writing it up in an autograph script, like a huge signature on a declaration of intent of old-fashioned service. Some of the descriptive phrases also echo a more leisurely time, for whoever in normal conversation calls a clothes shop a 'Hosier and Outfitter' or Mr Jones a 'High-Class Family Butcher'?

The best examples of really old shopfront lettering are behind glass, either painted or gilded directly on the back of the glass, or in the form of carved or indented lettering protected by glass. The latter are less likely to be the work of a local man than of one of the larger companies who specialised in this sort of work, like the Brilliant Sign Co of London, whose signs had a nationwide distribution. Either the lettering was carved into a plank of wood and gilded, or the words could be put together out of prefabricated pressed metal

---

This post-war banner is from Runcorn, and was painted by the famous firm of George Tutill who supplied a huge number of banners to churches, trade unions and friendly societies from the 1860s onwards. The scrollwork is arranged like heraldic mantling around the central 'shield' picture.

letters. The indented lettering was then gold-leafed whilst the back of the covering glass was painted all over except for the lettering, the gilded writing appearing through the painted glass panel which masked out the background. Gold and glass make for a long-lived partnership, but paint too, carefully applied to the back of glass, can last for a very long time, suffering nothing but a little fading. There are some immaculate pre-Second World War signs in existence which only give their age away by the dated style of the lettering. Signwriting on the inside of shop windows used to be very popular but there are few examples now, for most have suffered from the glass-writer's two main enemies, condensation and the over-zealous window cleaner. The best examples nowadays are usually found on glass fascia panels above the shop front, in particular above long-established butchers' shops which have pushed their 'high-class' image with the clean clarity of gold on glass.

There are few remnants left of the old sign-painters' trade, for the painting of pictorial signs or traditional symbols died in the face of competition from cheap colour poster printing and photography. One exception is of course pub sign work which tends to be done by artists specialising in that field or by breweries who maintain their own sign workshops, and with constant practice the standard is pretty high. However there are some traditional symbols and colour schemes that survive in shop decoration. Butcher's-shop paintwork, for example, was until quite recently always oak-grained or marbled, although red and white have now taken over in popularity in the freezer cabinet age. The butchers' symbol of a bull's head, however, keeps on recurring – as a pair of horns in the shop or on tiles on the wall, or in the work of the signwriter outside showing a bull's (or pig's) head flanking the owner's name on the fascia. It is a clear symbol that is prevalent right down the line, on the cattle trucks going to the slaughterhouse and on the sign at the farmer's gate. The sister sign of the

This sign company's shop in Hanley, Staffordshire, is almost a catalogue of popular lettering styles through the years since it was established in 1896. The fascia is a gilded carved board protected by painted glass and must surely date back to the early days of the company.

cow for the dairyman has now disappeared, as have the cream or white-painted corner shops that ran the small local milk rounds. Reminders of the reality of milk production are less productive than posters of pretty girls. Greengrocers still occasionally sport painted still-lifes of fruit, flowers and overflowing cornucopia on their mainly green shopfronts, but painted baskets of eggs with a sheaf of corn have gone with the old grocers who had bentwood chairs by the counter for the customers to sit on.

Most of the old signwriting books devote a small section to banner painting, either on silk for parades and pageantry, or on great cotton sign cloths to stretch across the street, advertising the pantomime or the summer fair. These are still in use, of course, but being of a temporary nature, they have less care spent on them than the traditional church or trade union banner which came out on every special occasion and had to last for years. Most of these were produced by commercial firms who specialised in such regalia, and the largest, George Tutill's of London, were estimated to have made at least three-quarters of the many thousands of banners that took to the streets between their heyday in the 1880s and the end of their production soon after the Second World War. There are still many in existence, and they are still used and honoured by the members; church parades and union

rally bring some beautiful examples of old painted design out on to modern streets. There is little difference between those that are a hundred years old and those that are only a youthful forty, for the same mixture of pious picture, acanthus scrollwork and signwritten ribbon was produced throughout the period – an amazing continuity of popular taste – and they still have the power to stir the heart and lift the spirit.

This surrealist pub sign from the *Four Alls* near Market Drayton in Shropshire is in a class of its own. The name is not uncommon throughout the country, sometimes known as the Five Alls or Six Alls, with a lawyer and a Devil who takes all, but the way the texts are painted in their own separate labels is very odd, slightly reminiscent of scriptural texts on the church wall of an earlier age. This strange mixture of pictorial work and abstract lettering design is now preserved within the pub, and is worth a pilgrimage.

The tiny stern cabin of a traditional horse-drawn narrow canal boat. *Bess* is a fine example of the lavish painted decoration common to these boats in their heyday, and the lettered name panel is a particularly good mix of fat decorated letters with scrolls and bordering, a decorative partner to the traditional castle painting alongside. (Photograph from the Harry Arnold Collection.)

Another well-documented and almost complete area of decorative signwriting is canal boat lettering, particularly that of the 'narrowboats' of the Midlands. The reasons for this amazing survival stem from the introduction of the railways in the mid-nineteenth century, when any new capital was poured into new railways, leaving the previously prosperous canals as the poor relation. They were still economically viable, but not attractive enough in profit terms to be developed or expanded significantly, and so remained largely unchanged. The same sized locks meant the same sized boats, and the same way of working them continued into the middle of the twentieth century. The canal boat people became a very tight-knit trade community, with the whole family involved, sometimes living in the tiny cabins in desperately over-crowded conditions. This almost inevitably led to the most awful social mess at one end of this separate society, with all the squalor of ignorance, vermin and disease, but it also created a very proud and independent group at the other end, setting themselves extremely high standards of cleanliness and ostentatious display, and developing what became a very individual style of boat decoration to bolster their self-esteem.

The boating community in general was able

to earn a reasonable living up to the first World War, including the few owner-boatmen and women who were helping to set these standards, and the best boat painting clearly reflects late-Victorian and Edwardian taste. Ornate decorated letters, coloured borders and mouldings, and the well-known roses and castle pictures gave a richness and expensive texture to what could practically only be a box cabin of limited size, showing strong similarities to the escapist baroque of the fairground. As competition from motor transport increased, and working hours were regulated between the wars, so the boat people became ever more anachronistic. However, they became equally determined to preserve their separate identity by demanding the continuation of their own traditions, and the ending of narrow-boat carrying in the 1960s saw the decorative conventions still alive and developing. Pleasure-boat and traditional-boat enthusiasts now try to preserve this way of life, but standards can slip very fast when the professionals cease to exert any control over what is acceptable and the souvenir industry takes over.

In a proper example of a well-painted canal boat there is a very happy integration of romantic imagination with utility. The intricate paintwork makes the small canal boat an object of pride and beauty, and something to be cared for, and thus makes the life that has to be led in it much easier to enjoy. The boat people could not compete with the rest of society in terms of quantity, because of the restricted size of the boat, but compensated with an extraordinary amount of surface quality.

Within this riot of decoration the signwriting became an important element. Lettering was chosen and developed to be as much part of the painted texture as the roses, with strongly contrasting tones and colours, clearly blocked out with all the associated shines, highlights and shadows. The face of the letter itself was rarely decorated, but a fancy letterstyle, or an Egyptian with plenty of excuses for two-coloured shading was favoured as it gave a

multi-coloured pattern to the panel that blended well with the other ingredients. Scrolled flourishes and painted flowers occupied the spaces between the words, and with lined borders and painted moulding, a narrow-boat cabin side panel was a fine example of pure decorative art.

It should be remembered that this extreme intensity of pattern making only applied to the boats of some of the smaller carrying companies and to some of the boats of the owner-boatmen. The great majority were owned and run by large transport firms, and although some made minor concessions to these traditions, most were looking for the least expensive minimum. A mainly black and white colour scheme, with the company name in block letters simply shaded like any other sign-writing of the time, was the standard desired by management, but the more domestic and fancy demands of the boat people working and living on the boats was a constant pressure, and as trade decreased there was actually a move towards more colour and more decoration among the surviving companies. Were they being kind to try and keep the best and most profitable crews until the end, or were they tempting the hard-working owner-boatmen to stay on the canal as they lost their own boats and traffic to the larger companies?

This scroll design is copied from the chimney decoration of a Leeds and Liverpool canal boat, whose traditional paintwork featured lots of scrolls, lines and colours as well as richly blocked and shaded lettering.

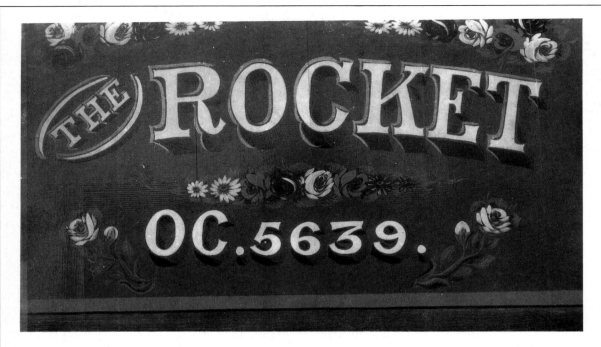

The amount of lettering on a narrow-boat is limited, but is displayed proudly. Canal by-laws insisted that the owner's and the boat's name were both clearly marked on each side. The company's name and address usually appeared on the panels of the stern cabin, with the boat's name on the top planks of the hull, sometimes carved into the woodwork in classical letter-cutting style. The development of steam and motor boats meant larger cabins to accommodate the engine, and the boat's name then also appeared on the cabin. The names chosen for the first steamboats in the late nineteenth century reflected the new mechanical muscle and superiority – *Monarch*, *Sultan* or *Queen* – and bold lettering filling the cabin panels accentuated this confidence. Both company name and boat name bridge the space in a shallow curve with lower lettering painted parallel with the bottom edge; this layout was the norm for many companies, both big and small, motor boats and horse boats. Extra phrases like 'Steerage Contractor' and canal and company numbers fill the centre space in a variety of scripts and italics, with scrollwork or flowers to finish the

An exaggerated Clarendon might best describe this canal boat letter-style, but years of practice have given it a personal handwritten directness. The light toned outline or highlight thrown round the upper side of the letter does not have much logic to it, but intensifies the pattern and adds another colour to make the lettering just as decorative as the painted flowers. This example is from the Braunston boatyard in Northamptonshire in about 1947. (Photograph by Barbara Jones.)

(Facing above) Frank Jones, seen here working at Leighton Buzzard on the Grand Union Canal in about 1950, was one of the most respected canal boat painters. His simple swelled end sans-serif lettering is heavily blocked out in two colours to create as much a pattern of letters as useful advertising. (Photograph from British Waterways Board Museum.)

(Facing below) Regular commercial cargo-carrying by narrow boat has now finished, but many of them continue in use as pleasure boats and many new ones have been built as cruisers. The lettering tradition also continues as on this recent example, signwritten by Bruce Tierson in a style developed from the work of one of the older Black Country canal tradesmen, Ted Chetwynd.

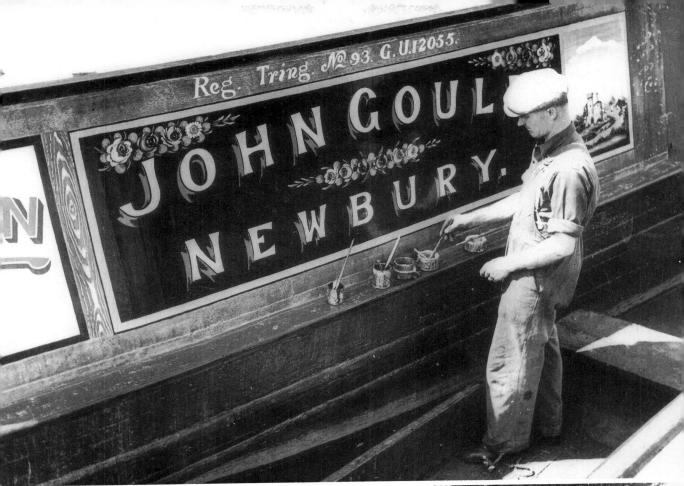

design in what became the standard narrow-boat style.

There were variations of course, and some owners tried to promote a much more up-to-date image by using contemporary layout and letterstyle, or used press advertising copy and design to extend their everyday advertising onto their transport. Firms like Cadbury's and Ovaltine did this, but it was the exception rather than the rule. For the majority, the texture and pattern of the old-fashioned signwriting and layout had a rightness for the job that made it appear impossible to improve until the end.

One of the factors that guided the development of the roses-and-castles tradition was the nature of the tradesmen who practised it, and the same factor applies to the lettering, often done by the same men. Although some of the larger boatyards and carriers brought in outsiders, much boat lettering was the work of boatbuilders, who regarded the painting of the boat as an extension of their trade. They were not professional signwriters or professional artists, so their work lacks that commercial polish that daily practice gives to the hand, but they did do it often enough to develop confidence, skill and personal style. Just as they were unable to make naturalistic paintings of flowers, and developed a decorative technique instead, so the lettering was some way from trade practice and a long way from classical ideals. Most of this naive work, whilst doing its job, was mediocre, but on the occasions when traditional and conventional paintwork was carried out by a naturally gifted but untrained artist, the result was folk art of the highest standard. The successful job provides a vehicle for the artistic needs of a whole group of people, a combination that satisfies the artistic instincts of the man who does it, the customer who pays for it, and the other consumer – the boating family who have to live with it and look after it. It's an old canal saying that 'if the paint's all right, the boat won't leak' – a boatman looking after his paintwork is looking after the company's boat as well.

Like narrow-boat lettering, fairground lettering is rarely part of the everyday work of an ordinary signwriter, but it does provide excellent illustrations of the potential of lettering as decorative art, often using it in an exciting and dramatic way, promoting its message visually rather than legibly, by design and colour more than by the words themselves. Most of the original design and painting work is carried out by specialist fairground firms, and the majority of the maintenance and repainting work is done by the showmen themselves, an amazingly talented bunch of people with a range of skills from heavy engineering to gold-leafing. Fairground work needs a long apprenticeship to assimilate the many techniques, colours and designs that make up the showground language of decoration. There are elements surviving from the Victorian age, from art deco of the jazz era, and from Teddy boy rock'n'roll, all combined with an awareness of the popular image of the immediate present, which is splendidly confusing. There is a willingness to try new, modern things, but only if they can be couched in the familiar fairground mode, a paradox that results in a mad third period of imagery between past and present that belongs to the fairground alone.

The lettering shows this variation of origin as soon as the superficial cohesion of style is analysed. Still exerting a strong influence is the Victorian and Edwardian exuberance of carving and gilding that was the hallmark of the fair at its peak of popularity, and Louis XV-style carving, either painted to look like the real thing, or in the form of abstract scrolls, is still a major feature. The letter shape that echoes this most eloquently is the Tuscan style, with its burgeoning leaf serifs and uncurling growths for centre strokes, well suited to the jungle motif that occurred regularly in the past and the acanthus leaf of classical architecture. Very often this leafy letter is growing up out of another more rigid form, so that the top half is in one style and the lower half in another, and the midway junction becomes an extra decorative feature, an extra

Visual poetry by Lloyd Holland, an extraordinary piece of modern fairground expressionism on a Helter Skelter from north-west England.

line of pattern along the centre of a word. This already elaborate letter is then enriched by 'bringing-it-up' as a three-dimensional object, painting the thickness much more realistically than is usual in signwritten work, with every excuse for shading and highlighting at its decorative ultimate. The object is to achieve the richness of an imagined Palace of Versailles blended with the tropically exotic, the words less important than texture. A favourite place for this style is on the rounding boards at the top of a roundabout, especially as the surviving gallopers quite blatantly promote their appeal by nostalgia, but it turns up on other rides and stalls less obviously suitable. Today the fairground is probably the only place

where this form of letter can be used with genuine comfort – an expression of escapist enjoyment, for those unaffected by educated 'good taste', that has far outlived its fashion and become a firm popular art favourite.

The period between the wars was a new fairground era. The internal combustion engine had come of age and was proving itself on land and in the air, and images of speed vied with the old aristocratic opulence for popularity with the paying customer. Motor cars and bikes arrived, both as rides on the dodgems or speedway roundabout and as pictures on the high front boards over the entrance. Racing cars and aeroplanes now roar out at us from the surrounding scrollwork, and angled abstract patterns of lightning and polite cubism fill the panels between the renaissance pillars. The lettering becomes sharper and clearer, crisply outlined footed roman

119

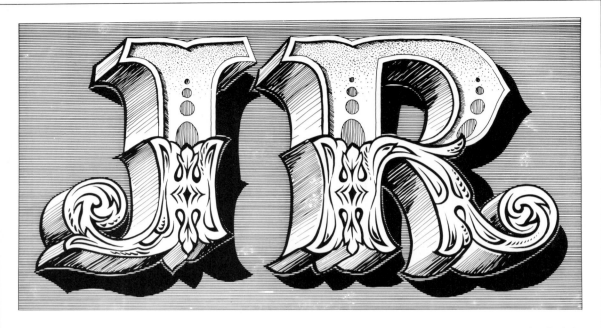

Fairground fantasy, an ornate Tuscan letter-form taken beyond legibility to expressive nostalgia.

with a dropped shadow proudly presenting the owner's name, or big block letters shooting out from a deep central vanishing point, the face painted as if pressed out of chrome plated metal – the crystal facets of art deco pushed out by mass production. But still the 1890s persist, and old fashioned Tuscan can turn up anywhere.

Since the Second World War the tendency has been towards a simpler basic letter-form, but a more expressive layout. A fast fairground script has developed, that whips across the panel like a ribbon in a wind, often tangled into the scrolls that surround it. It may actually be joined-up writing, or just overlapping freely drawn capitals, but the overriding intention is to describe the nature of the movement of the modern ride that it is advertising – the Whip, Waltzer, Swirl, or Cyclone Twist. Although the letter shape may be simple, the treatment rarely is. It might be an outline letter, with the centre recessed and painted in a sweet-paper design of metallic stars or coloured stripes. It

will certainly be blocked out and shaded in strongly contrasting colours so that every simple direction line is echoed several times in several colours, and the cross strokes of E or A and the tail of the R may lick across neighbouring letters without logic.

One man helped to shape this modern style more than any other, a prolific and talented professional fairground decorator called Fred Fowle, from London, whose death in 1984 was a sad blow to the business. Happily, his work and life have been well-documented, and masses of his paintwork still travels the fairs, a strong influence on his successors. He carried on and developed the style of painting and decorating that he learnt as an apprentice in the 1930s at Lakins, a very well-known firm in London, but introduced many new ideas as he developed his own business after the War. He used brighter colours than anyone had used before, in stronger combinations; he introduced new images from the cinema and advertising, and twisted the old signwriter's ribbon idea into a writhing explosion of line and colour, an ornamental image in its own right. Most of all he was a master of lettering and scrollwork. He blended the Footed Roman of the inter-war years, with its angled cutaway block serifs, with 'Swash' capitals, where any serif or arm of a letter could sweep out into a flourish; he then combined these two with his painted version of the old acanthus scroll to produce spectacular lettering designs. Borders and surrounds used all the influences of the century from marbled pillars to tigers and space ships, but in some of his work the pictorial image disappeared altogether, and the word became the image, a forceful use of lettering as fine decorative art.

He pioneered several surface patterns on the face of the letter, of hearts, stripes and diamonds, and experimented with lots of different letter styles, modern and traditional,

with varying degrees of success. One satisfying example is his treatment of the name 'Silcocks' in the illustration on page 123, where the combined parts make up a complete letter, but whose individual parts alone would be virtually unreadable. Fancy signwriting usually begins with a recognisable letterform, however grotesque or reshaped, that can be painted in and spaced correctly as a first step, then enriched to the desired degree with outlining, blocking out and decorative infilling. Here, however, the underlying letter is really invisible, just suggested by the outline and shading, with the details hinted at by the centre decoration. It was, of course, worked out on paper first, and as this panel is used as a repeat pattern a strong pounce design was needed, but it is beautifully designed for the craftsman's brush and spraygun. With the parts combined the name swings flamboyantly across with just the right mixture of pride, glamour and temptation, a masterpiece for an exciting fairground ride!

Every trick of the fairground painter's book is employed on these Helter Skelter porch panels by Fred Fowle of London. Marbling, scrolls, ribbons and shadows, and a total mastery of lettering that allows him to do what he likes with it, with great success! Knutsford Royal May Day Fair, 1985.

One of a whole set of signboards painted around 1960 by a Mr Winnot from Ashton-under-Lyne. They had several homes before gracing Mrs Hill's round stall, photographed here at Cartmel races, 1984. The basic letter shape is rounded out and shadowed with a spray gun before being finished with a vigorous brushstroke pattern that links it with the stylised scroll-work round the edge.

(Facing) The signature of a master craftsman of the fair – Fred Fowle's treatment of Silcock's famous name.

7

Crossroads or DEAD END?

THE TRADITION TODAY

ALTHOUGH it is good to see old-fashioned signwriting still surviving in different areas, the true health of a traditional trade has to be judged by how well it adapts to a changing world without altering out of all recognition, and how successfully it can do new jobs in a time-honoured way. The loss of the old apprenticeship system will influence it, for it will be very much more the responsibility of the individual man or woman to maintain standards and use traditional methods. There are a number of areas where the customer will probably continue to search out painters who can supply the traditional product because it suits the nature of the business. Pubs and breweries would seem to be good clients for the foreseeable future; and the church still shows some of the signwriters' finest efforts, often done as gifts to their own parish and as much worship as work. The office doorways and alleyways around the Inns of Court in London are smothered in fine signwritten roman lettering which has been a tradition with the lawyers for generations, and shows little sign of disappearing. Fishing boats may not need much lettering, but the fisherman expects the name of his boat to be expressed with considerable love and respect, as befits the cockleshell craft he trusts his life to – and there may be a similar feeling underlying the care that is bestowed on

some modern lorries. Traditions are still growing there.

It is a little unexpected to find traditional signwriting, never mind real folk art, in a fast-moving and growing modern industry, but road haulage provides some interesting examples. One reason for discussing canal transport in such depth is that road transport has many parallel features, and is developing more. Like boating, lorry driving is becoming a subculture with its own private traditions, with painting and signwriting as a significant part. Both trades are about long-distance transport, and the painting reflects the operator's attitude to the job and the tool for doing it – the boat or lorry. In both cases the tradesmen operate in specialised worlds, with a practice and skill that sets them apart as a trade community. In the past the big difference that set the canal boatman apart from everyone else was that he not only worked the boat but lived on it as well with his whole family. The boat or barge was not just a tool for doing the transport job, but his home too. Long-distance lorry drivers have

Old-fashioned respect for the law expressed in traditional letter-forms in London, where respectability and security is still handpainted in the style of the Victorian age, happily with little sign of change to come.

always been expected to stay away from home over several nights, but the introduction of the sleeper-cab into Britain has made the driver's lorry much more personalised, and it is not now unusual for a driver to live in his lorry for a couple of weeks at a time, even on internal British routes. The similarities are suddenly much clearer.

Like the boats, the general treatment of lorry paintwork can be broadly sub-divided into groups, for only a relatively small proportion fits within the interest of this book. Most numerous are the trucks belonging to very large impersonal transport consortia, or to manufacturers and distributors where the colour scheme and layout is an extension of the company's corporate identity, an image designed by a graphic artist in an advertising studio. The colours of Tesco's or Sainsbury's wagons belong as much to the transport tradition as do their plastic bags, and although they

Flamboyant confidence on a Northumberland fishing boat from Amble. The fishing fleet is smaller than it used to be, but the dogged pride is the same, and bright colours and powerful graining still shout defiance from the fishermen, and romance to the landlubber. Decoration and lettering by Lawrence Henderson.

'Walking Days', when the Sunday Schools parade their banners, still continue in a few places, but this banner from Runcorn, Cheshire, ended its public life in 1975 when its home church was demolished for redevelopment. It probably dates from before the Second World War, a lovely balanced composition of signwriting, ribands, scrolls and picture, but the yellow brocade round the picture is a later strengthening, for it is now very frail.

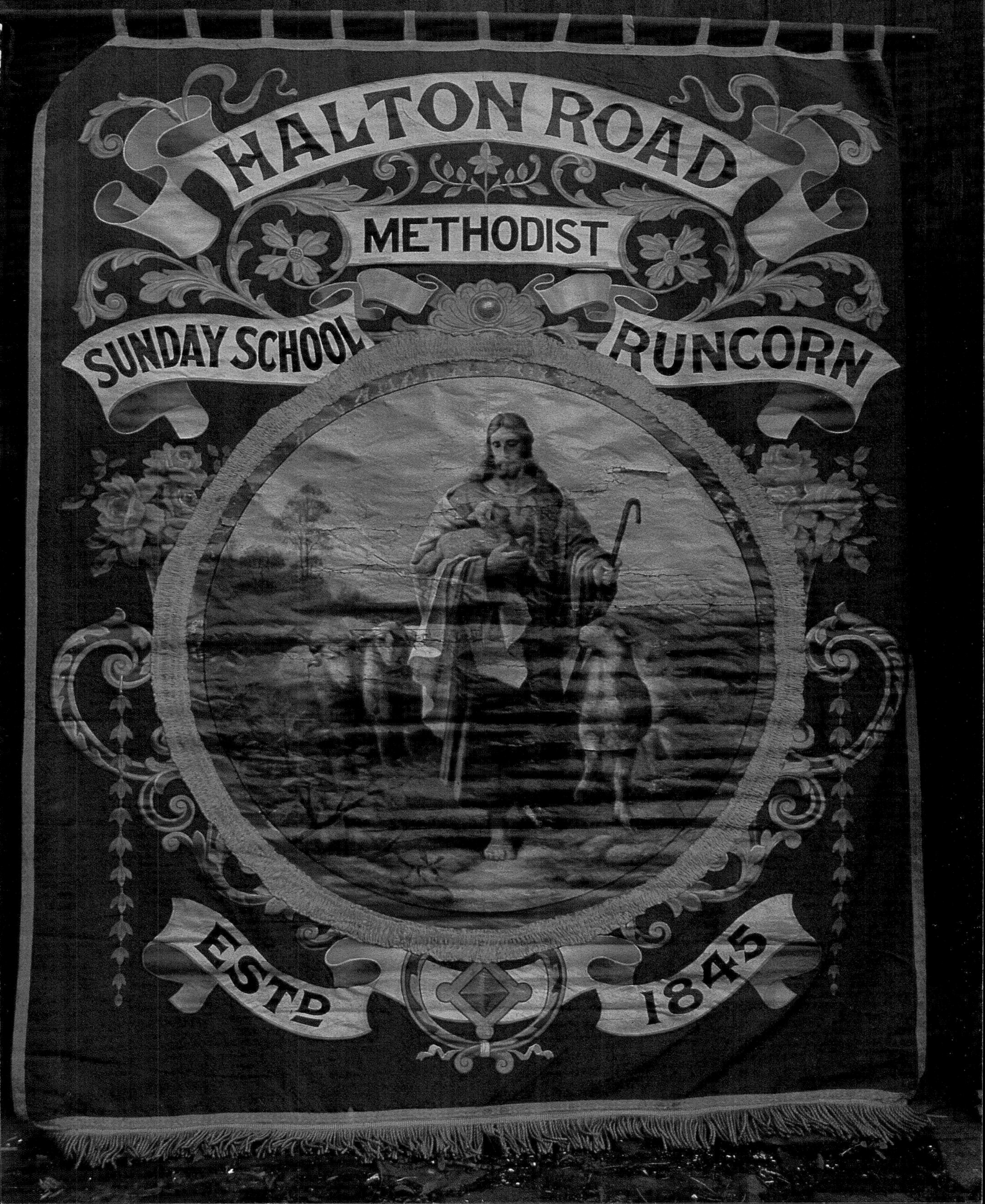
HALTON ROAD
METHODIST
SUNDAY SCHOOL
RUNCORN
ESTD
1845

require the skills of coachpainter and sign-writer, there is no room for personal interpretation or art. There is also a very large number of vehicles that remain in the manufacturers' colours, as supplied ex-works, or that are resprayed in one colour only for cheapness and efficiency with the simplest possible addition of the company name. The remaining part of the road haulage industry is only a small proportion, but it is still a very large number of vehicles, from companies with a hundred wagons down to those with one or two. It is these firms that preserve, perhaps unconsciously, the traditions of a time-tested trade, as well as encouraging the most interesting new developments that reflect the drivers' tastes and aspirations.

Paintwork can be roughly divided into traditional and trucking. The former is of most interest from the signwriting point of view, but the image of the American truck has been a fast-growing influence, and is increasingly popular. The development of our motorways, with the subsequent increase in tonnage and new continental traffic, has brought British road transport far closer to the American pattern, with larger lorries and longer distances involved. Sleeper cabs with a bunk, television and other home comforts are now quite normal. Not surprisingly the flashy customising of the American truck has now found an echo in Britain, and the multi-coloured 'go-faster' stripes of Macks and Peterbilts blend with the modern styling of Scanias and Leylands quite comfortably. Add chrome-plated exhaust stacks, curtains and miniature flags in the cab window and you have a proud British trucker – a word quite foreign to English roads twenty years ago – reflecting the changes in the job and the worker. Extreme examples of lorry customising are still rare, but they set standards that many drivers

The classic layout of lettering on this lorry cab door is very similar to the usual one on canal boat cabins, with the owner's name arched over the home town, but the decorative scroll and coach lining around the panels are direct descendants of horse-drawn vehicle coach painting.

quietly aspire to, or secretly envy, and few cabs do not have some ornaments from that private truck driver's world.

These modern additions fit snugly into what I have called the 'traditional' style of wagon-painting as well, and it is because it has adapted, whilst retaining its original character that it has a special value above mere fashion. It seems a good test of popular taste when a style of vehicle decoration can remain recognisably the same for a hundred years and still be used in the modern world without appearing twee or quaint – qualities for which lorry-drivers are not usually noted.

Colour is the keynote, deep rich colours with red and blue leading in popularity, blue bodywork with bright red undercarriage and

Mr Kirk's cattle truck from Macclesfield, Cheshire, boldly continues all the livestock transport traditions of graining, colour, monograms and pictures. Coachpainting by Saxons of Sandbach.

wheels, or perhaps a red and maroon cab with blue mudguards. Centre bands or door panels may be in a paler shade, or a complementary tone of a different colour, pale blue with a darker green or cream with brown, or each section separately panelled with a border of contrasting colour. In all cases the final finish is coach lining, thin lines of white or cream outlining and highlighting each panel of body-work, with fancy loops or quadrants at the corners. There is no sense of streamlining in this approach, stressing as it does the sepa-rateness of the component parts, and it asks to be admired as a static group, quite unlike the yankee banding which is far more active, based on speed and power in motion.

As an extension to the lining, some firms have scrolls painted in the panels or one of the designs made up of shallow curves, that are simple to do with a long-haired lining brush, seen at their most complicated on the shafts of horse-drawn vehicles. These designs still fol-low the pattern of the lining that 'picked out' the chamfering of wooden vehicles of the past, from mail-coach to milkman's float, and fol-lowing the connection back from lining to colour, it is no big surprise to discover that the commonest colour scheme for nineteenth-century farm wagons was a deep blue body with red wheels. Farmers often acted as carriers in country districts, recouping some of the capital costs of an expensive wagon and horses by becoming transport contractors in slack times, and it seems possible that many turned to road transport full-time. Certainly

S. J. Bargh is a company typical of many in road haulage, with an affection for the past showing through their hard modern business approach to the present. Their modern motorway trucks, coachpainted in two shades of green, are still signwritten in a traditional style that does not look out of place on their old immaculately restored vintage petrol lorry, seen in the top picture parked on their depot forecourt as the best sort of advert. It was signwritten by Ray Manning of Preston, seen in the lower picture writing a new wagon in December 1985.

some long-distance lorry firms have grown in more recent times from short-haul agricultural or livestock merchants, and there is a strong connection between town and country, agri-culture and industry in the transport business. The strong bright colours, specially made by paint manufacturers as 'transport' colours have a long history in popular taste.

The main space for signwriting is on the cab door. The three basic layouts discussed before recur again; horizontal lines of parallel letter-ing, a diagonal name striking across in script like a signature, and most reminiscent of canal boats, the company name arched above the address written horizontally below it. Lettering will be blocked out in strong contrasting colours and could be in any letterform from simple Block to Blackletter. Gold lettering used to be the favourite finish, outlined with black and shaded, but this is now rare. Tele-phone and telex numbers are useful items to fill in the asymmetrical shape of cab doors, and can be bent and twisted into corners to finish the layout. Flourishes and scrollwork sometimes appear to enrich the design, but the use of varying letterforms within the message, and painted ribbons to accentuate certain words are the main elements that give it an old-fashioned quality and richness that is unusual elsewhere.

A phrase such as 'Haulage Contractor' often appears as well, quite unnecessarily consider-ing it is painted on the side of a lorry, but expressing the pride within the trade as much as advertising outside it. As a descriptive phrase it can be in more expressive lettering, often in beautiful copperplate, or painted on a separate ribbon, and becomes a proud label for driver and owner alike. This area of the business is run by men who know it from the bottom up as many of them started as owner-drivers themselves, and there is no culture barrier between boss and workman. Their tastes in transport styles are broadly similar and both are proud of the continuity, although they are constantly absorbing new influences.

The growth of sports sponsorship, for

example, as a means of advertising has made changes. In motor racing the pattern of the large lettering has merged with streamlining stripes to produce an extraordinary new image of speed – a vehicle smothered in sponsor's name and advertising stickers, an explosive pattern of lettering and brash colours. This has had its effect on truck fashions, both traditional and modern, and lettering has increased in size and has spread to any vacant space on the cab, not so much for what it says as what it does, adding texture and an atmosphere of successful commercial dash. It also gives the gifted signwriter a broader field in which to work. Some drivers have always given an individual name to their vehicle, but it has become more common recently to see this personal name delicately written in a flowing script over the radiator cap or in the centre of the bumper. Names vary, from the poetic to the mundane – 'Lily of the Valley' to 'Marge', or 'Queen of the Road' to 'Alf' – and sometimes overlap with the drivers 'handle' or citizens' band radio call-up name.

Images from heraldry get a lot of use in truck painting, often incorrectly if not illegally used, but decoratively satisfying. Many use the British emblems of the constituent countries – Welsh dragons and feathers, Scottish thistles and the English rose – and the Royal Garter has been shamelessly stolen to frame monograms or fleet and telephone numbers on the front wings. County emblems feature, the red rose of Lancaster or the Staffordshire knot, but it is flags that have made the biggest impact recently, especially since the growth of inter-national ferry traffic. Scottish firms have often made use of St Andrew's cross, with the word Scotland over the cab, but there has been a large increase in the use of the Union Jack, particularly since the Silver Jubilee, as a proud emblem of patriotism and free enterprise, and this certainly suits the way road transport sees itself. The range of ingredients available to the signwriter to finish off a lorry's paintwork is now excitingly wide, provided the customer can be persuaded to pay. Lucky for this lively popular art form, many are prepared to do so.

Changing fashions of vehicle painting are reflected very fast in the coach trade, for their greatest sales boast has always been to offer the latest improvements on the most up-to-date luxury vehicles. The arrival in this country of the American trucking colours has had a significant effect, and most firms have dropped the old two-tone streamlining in favour of bands of colour spraying out along the sides of the coach, changing direction violently like a multi-coloured section of a lightning flash. However sharp the image, the operators still rely on high-quality lettering to promote a sense of reliable service and dependability; the boot door often bears signwriting of very high quality, interspersed with sprays of flags to give a hint of international travel excitement, although it might never go further than the North Wales coast.

Another sub-division of road haulage with its own coach-painting conventions is livestock transport such as cattle wagons and horse boxes. The front of the Luton body, the box that extends forward over the cab proper, is a prime place for the name and trade, but it often bears a symbol or portrait of the business as well, a painting of prize cattle or sheep, or a single bull's head, still the regular sign of the butcher. Lettering may follow any of the usual patterns on the doors and bodywork, but the cab itself, quite clearly of pressed metal, is sometimes beautifully grained in two contrasting wood finishes – oak and mahogany perhaps – with red bumpers and wheels. It

The development of the sleeper cab with a cross bunk behind the driver's seat has resulted in an extra panel of bodywork on the outside, available for more lettering or in this case the Mackintosh arms. The autograph script across the door has a very old-fashioned conservative style to it, but Volvo's own name emblazoned on the cab corners has the feel of modern commercial motor-racing sponsorship. Both styles are blending together in the developing traditions of truck painting.

Superb signwork in black and white in Bridport, Dorset; a town well worth visiting just for the large amount of good signwriting on public display.

The livery of this Bedford livestock wagon is from the coachpainting firm of Saxons of Sandbach in Cheshire who, with a few other companies in this part of the country, specialises in this high-quality work. The cab itself, so obviously pressed metal, is grained with two contrasting wood finishes, with bright red mudguards and wheels, with more rich colour added by the name ribbon, and some elegant roman lettering. Careful varnishing can preserve work like this for a very long time, for the vehicles themselves rarely do a huge mileage compared to normal road haulage, and it seems to be a small painting tradition which is safe for the near future.

used to be done to match up with the varnished wooden bodywork of the best cattle-truck makers, but has now become a tradition on its own, quite illogical but wonderful, satisfying the basic need for extra quality in everyday life. It is a visible example of the human pleasure in making things more beautiful than they need to be, expressed in a form that everybody can enjoy.

One of the more mundane reasons that signwriting has such a strong hold on road transport, vans as well as trucks and buses, is that vehicle bodywork is generally curved, and the styling is altered and updated every few years. It is difficult to screenprint or apply transfers to double-curved surfaces, and it is expensive to prepare them for just a few vehicles, so here too the signwriter appears to have a secure future in the more discriminating part of the market.

Flat signwork, however, is more of a problem, and more likely to disappear. Many modern signs are made from translucent plastic, and are internally lit, the successors to the neon of the 1930s, using cut-out letters stuck to a background sheet. The fact that odd letters drop off after a few years is no great drawback as mergers or the frenetic updating of the corporate image makes longevity in the old-fashioned sense less important.

This elaborate pavement board by John Wagon of Teignmouth, Devon, has a colourful, personal and humorous style that seems just right for a holiday town café, whether it rains or not. It is individual and quite obviously the work of one person with a paintbrush, and while customers can be found willing to pay for complicated work like this the signwriting tradition will carry on adapting to the future.

———————

There is terrific potential for modern signs, but it would be sad if too much has to be displaced to make room for the new, both physically and 'spiritually'. There are good signs and fine craftsmanship in plastic, but the availability of a limited line of off-the-shelf letters, usually in a letterform designed for print, means the signmaker has his design options severely curtailed. It will always make commercial sense to use what is easily available instead of designing each job anew, and the temptation to yet more standardisation is strong. The signwriters' hand-painted letters, however good or bad, are at least infinitely variable to suit any space or any colour scheme. This possible variation does not of course guarantee a good sign, but it does make it an individual creation. Interesting failures are perhaps preferable to bland acceptability spreading everywhere. But then the great strength of working within a tradition or convention is that it cushions the popular artist from disasters. When he is working within a tradition he is leaning on a couple of hundred years of experience both from his artistic forbears and his customers. Let's hurry forward more slowly.

A PRACTICAL ✝ TREATISE UPON GILDING,

⌇ BY EZRA HOYLE. ⌇

SCIENCE IS FACT.   TO APPLY IS ART.

The Art and Science of Bright Gilding upon Glass, Japan-ware, Wood, China, or any other Hard Surface,

BY **EZRA HOYLE**, THE ORIGINAL,

Inventor and Patentee of the Process for Manipulating Gold Leaf.

Eclipse GOLD SIZE, Unsurpassable, per Bottle 5/-

Established over 40 years as Designer, Decorator, Glass and Sign Writer to the Trade.

E. H. having had a very extended experience in the above-mentioned branches, gives instructions in conjunction with his newly improved Glass Gilding Size, of which he is the sole manufacturer, with the assurance that those who carry out the directions cannot possibly fail to succeed. Not only is it the simplest, cheapest, and most practical method for the student, but to the experienced workman it is an equally valuable aid.

E. H. has devoted himself to the study of every accessible formula and process without discovering one that clearly elucidates the objects aimed at, except his *Compound Eclipse Gold Size*. The artist is, after studying most methods, left in a state of doubt, and with a very incomplete knowledge of the art of Practical Glass Gilding, etc.

147, Manningham Lane, Bradford, Yorks.

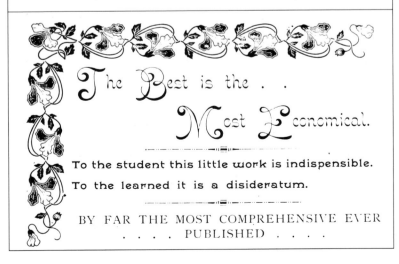

The Best is the . . Most Economical.

To the student this little work is indispensible.

To the learned it is a disideratum.

BY FAR THE MOST COMPREHENSIVE EVER . . . . PUBLISHED . . . .

Pages from a booklet published prior to 1930

Bibliography

PART 1: PRACTICAL BOOKS

Pᴿᴬᴄᴛɪᴄᴀʟ books about signwriting, arranged in chronological order. This is as complete as I can make it, and includes a number of titles noted from library catalogues which I have been unable to trace, but there are bound to be more, especially if one includes American books. I have excluded books of alphabets even when they include the word 'signwriter' in the title, for they are all equally useful or useless depending on the reader's viewpoint or experience. Nearly all general painting and decorating manuals also include a chapter on lettering, and the books directed at the ticket and show card writer also have some relevance to signwriting, but in this list I have regarded it as a separate trade. Some of the books listed are now quite rare and difficult to find, and I add my own critical comments, with trepidation, to help the reader judge which ones might be worth following up, for his or her own research.

1827 Whittock, Nathaniel. *The Decorative Painter and Glazier's Guide* (London, G. Virtue)
He never uses the word 'signwriter' but does give some lettering advice to sign painters. It is not very good advice, but the book is a fascinating glimpse at the various jobs of the decorative artist of the period.
1852 Barber, Edmund. *The Painters', Grainers' and Writers' Assistant* (London. H. Elliot)
A hundred-page pamphlet of recipes for paints and varnishes, and instructions for graining and marbling. The two pages on 'Writing' are mainly about gilding and suitable colour schemes for lettering.
1854 Sutherland, William. *The Grainer, Marbler, and Signwriter's Assistant*
Not seen.
1860 Sutherland, William. *The Practical Guide to Sign Writing and Gilding, and Ornamenting on Glass* (Birmingham, Thomas Underwood)
A large-format book with five pages of text, an engraved diagram and six lithographed plates, mainly of additional decoration and heraldry, but there is one page of good alphabets and one good colour plate of large, elaborately decorated letters. The second of a series of books whose influence stretches well into the next century.
1871 Callingham, James. *Signwriting and Glass Embossing* (Simpkin Marshal, reprinted 1874 and 1880)
Rather verbose but a good practical book of the time. Very good on colours, but has only a few diagrams in black and white.
1875 Davidson, Ellis A. *Practical Manual of Housepainting, Graining, Marbling and Signwriting* (5th ed. London, Crosby Lockwood, 1888. Reprinted many times up to at least 1947)
His self-opinionated pedantic style makes it difficult to believe it was so popular, but it is quite thorough.
1879 Badenoch, James Greig. *The Art of Letter-painting Made Easy* (London, C. Lockwood.

Reprinted until at least 1929)

A beginner's booklet about setting out lettering on a numbered block system.

1889 Sutherland, William. *The Art and Craft of Signwriting* (Manchester, Decorative Arts Journal Co. Facsimile reprint, Omega, 1987)

An updated version of the 1860 book with much learnt from the intervening authors. 26 colour plates of alphabets and ornament.

1890 *The Standard Signwriter's and Lettering Companion* (New York, Strong)

Compiled and published by an association of practical sign painters. Not seen.

1898 Sutherland W. and W. G. *The Sign Writer and Glass Embosser* (Manchester, Decorative Arts Journal Co, and London, Simpkin, Marshall, Hamilton, Kent)

Expanded version of the 1889 book with extra chapters and extra colour plates. A superb collector's item.

1914 Hasluck, Paul N. (ed.). *How to Write Signs, Tickets and Posters* (London, Cassell)

'Work' handbook series. Good, small, readable, and still a useful book.

1916 Dowling, Henry George. *Painters' and Decorators' Work* (London, George Routledge)

Only one chapter on signwriting, but several attractive line illustrations.

1922 Hasluck, Paul N. (ed.). *Glass Writing, Embossing and Fascia Work* (publisher not known)

Not seen.

1923 Sutherland, W. G. (ed.). *The Modern Signwriter.* (Manchester, Decorative Arts Journal Co) Republished until at least 1954. A very useful series of articles by various contributors. Became the 'standard' work until the 1960s.

1935 Bell, Stanley. *Modern Ticket and Sign Writing* (London, W. Foulsham)

Poor. Interesting only for very dated examples of lettering and layouts.

1935 Birtles, T. G. *Signwriting* (New York, The Studio Limited)

One of the 'Hours of Leisure' series. Simplistic beginner's book, suggesting signwriting as a hobby. Almost as much about painting the board as painting lettering.

1937 Coates, W. H. *Van Writing Up to Date* (London, Blandford, revised second ed. 1949)

Still a good practical book.

1949 Duvall, Edward J. *Modern Sign Painting* (Illinois, USA, Frederick J. Drake)

A pleasant, direct book. Some clear alphabets, and interesting photographs of American style signs.

1950 Atkinson, Frank J. *Atkinson's Sign Art* (Jackson, Mississippi, USA, Stanley Ruff)

Very personalised instruction section, an old man decrying the present. Some interesting designs offered, but more 1910 than 1950.

1953 Hearn, B. *The Art of Signwriting* (London, B. T. Batsford)

An attractive, clear, useful book. Recommended.

1961 Le Blanc, Raymond J. *Gold Leaf Techniques for the Signwriter* (Cincinnati, USA, Signs of the Times, 3rd printing 1978)

Very clear practical instructions, well illustrated with photos.

1984 Stewart, Bill. *Signwork, A Craftsman's Manual* (London, Collins)

Excellent in all respects, and hopefully available for many years to come.

PART 2: GENERAL BIBLIOGRAPHY

Ayres, James. *British Folk Art* (London, Barrie and Jenkins, 1977)

Bartram, Alan. *Fascia Lettering in the British Isles; Street Name Lettering in the British Isles; Tombstone Lettering in the British Isles* (all published by Lund Humphries, 1978) Published in one volume as *The English Lettering Tradition from 1700 to the Present Day* (London, Lund Humphries, 1986)

British Institute of Industrial Art. *The Art of Lettering and its Use in Diverse Crafts and Trades,* Committee report. (Oxford University Press, 1931)

Catich, E. M. *The Origin of the Serif* (Davenport, Iowa, USA, Catfish Press, 1968)

Evans, Bill, and Lawson, Andrew. *A Nation of Shopkeepers* (London, Plexus Publishing, 1981)

Evetts, L.C. *Roman Lettering* (London, Pitman, 1938)

Fletcher, Geoffrey S. *Popular Art in England* (London, George G. Harrap, 1962)

Gorman, John. *Banner Bright* (London, Allen Lane, 1973) Revised and enlarged edition (Buckhurst Hill, Essex, Scorpion, 1986)

Gray, Nicolete. *Lettering on Buildings* (London, Architectural Press, 1960)

Heal, Sir Ambrose. *London Tradesmen's Cards of the Eighteenth Century* (Cambridge University Press, 1925)

The English Writing Masters and their Copy Books 1570–1800 (Cambridge University Press, 1931)

Jones, Barbara. *The Unsophisticated Arts* (London, Architectural Press, 1951)

Lambert, M. and Marx, Enid. *English Popular Art* (London, B. T. Batsford, 1951)

Lancaster, John. *Lettering Techniques* (London, B. T. Batsford, 1980)

Larwood, J. and Hotten, J. C. *History of Signboards* (London, Chatto and Windus, 1866)

Murphy, John. *Irish Shopfronts* (Northern Ireland, Appletree Press, 1981)

Sutton, James. *Signs in Action* (London, Studio Vista, 1965)

Weedon, Geoff, and Ward, Richard. *Fairground Art* (London, White Mouse Editions, 1981)

Whitbread. *Inn-Signia* (London, Whitbread and Co Ltd, 1948)

PART 3: MAGAZINES AND CATALOGUES

Architectural Review. March 1953. Article about John Hume, signwriter of Kelso by C. Forehoe. Many other editions mention lettering and signwriting in relation to buildings.

Decorators and Painters Magazine. Monthly copies between 1910 and 1917 contain little snippets of information, too numerous to catalogue separately.

Fairground Mercury. The regular journal of the Fairground Association of Great Britain always contains some material relating to fairground decoration. See winter edition of 1983–84, 'Fred Fowle: Portrait of the Master'.

Journal of Decorative Art, edited by W. G. Sutherland. First published in 1880, contains much of interest about the high-class decorating trade, with occasional references to signwriting.

Motif. Winter 1963–64 contains 'English Vernacular', a study in traditional letter forms by James Mosley. Excellent.

Signs. Trade catalogue published by the Brilliant Sign Company of London in about 1939. Little on handpainted signs, but very good on pressed metal letters and neon, with many useful photographs.

Index

Numbers in *italics* refer to illustrations